Michael Kunz

Dressage
from Medium
to Grand Prix

Dressage from Medium to Grand Prix

Recognising and correcting problems

By Michael Kunz

Copyright © of original edition 2006 by Cadmos GmbH, Brunsbek
Copyright © of this edition 2006 by Cadmos Equestrian
Translated by: Konstanze Allsopp
Typesetting and design: Ravenstein + Partner, Verden
Cover photograph: Arnd Bronkhorst
Drawings: Maria Mähler
Printers: Westermann Druck, Zwickau

Printed in Germany

ISBN 978-3-86127-924-2

Contents

Contents

Contents

Introduction

In my many years working as a professional (German) Fédération National (FN) riding instructor and dressage trainer, I repeatedly meet riders who can only describe the visible outward form of dressage movements. Often they have no well-grounded background knowledge regarding, for example, the precise preparations and the aids, and as a result of this faults occur during the execution of the movements and, in many cases, it also leads to overall problems in the training of the horse.

This book offers dressage riders, who have acquired the necessary skill level for medium dressage to Grand Prix, comprehensive descriptions of the most important movements which are demanded in the dressage tests of the Deutsche Reiterliche Vereinigung (FN) from the medium level upward. The detailed presentations for the correct execution are aimed at giving the reader a more in-depth theoretical understanding and, on this basis, at the same time serve as instructions for their practical transformation.

None of the exercises of the classical school of dressage stands alone; each movement is a means to an end, builds upon other exercises practised before, and in turn serves as a preparation for further training. In this manner, movements should be regarded as tools which, similar to a craftsman's tools, can be used to perform certain tasks. Each movement sets focal points that the rider can use to exert an influence on the horse for purposeful further training, as well as for use as corrective measures.

It is, no doubt, unnecessary to concentrate on faults in this book, which inevitably occur in the case of an insufficient basic training of the rider and horse. A mastery of the rider's foundations – a relaxed, correct dressage seat, the basic correct application of the aids and a well developed sensitivity in the seat – is as much a self-evident prerequisite for further dressage training for competitive and hobby riding as a "durchlässiges" (often translated as supple) horse that has been trained systematically. Faults, on the other hand, that are typical for the respective movement described and that, for different reasons, occur repeatedly during practice for the achievement of the movement, are discussed intensively in this book, and are presented in direct context with ways and means to correct them.

As a number of lessons are similar with regard to preparation, execution and correction of faults, it is inevitable that repetitions will occur – in fact they are definitely desired in order to elucidate the close correlation between the individual movements. In addition, I thought it important to describe each movement very precisely and comprehensively in order to spare the rider from having to seek complicated references to other parts of the book and thereby having to search backwards and forwards through the pages.

I distance myself explicitly from training methods that ignore the physiological prerequisites and psychological basic requirements of the horse, which attempt to achieve supposedly artistic movements with technical aids that are contrary to animal welfare and are executed in a form of short-cut procedures. The most important requirements in the course of the entire training are respect and humbleness towards the horse. These reward the rider who proceeds down the, maybe slightly longer, road of a truly classical training with a co-operative sports partner who reacts to the lightest aids and remains healthy in the process.

The high goal of classical dressage is a well-exercised horse that presents itself in harmony and balance in graceful, straight, powerful, balanced demonstration. Without the correct execution of the movements, a rider will not be able to bring out this "becoming more beautiful", this aesthetic presentation of the horse. Hence the goal is the road towards the end!

Michael Kunz

Shoulder-in

If the movement is being executed correctly, an observer will see a horse with good elevated carriage. The horse will be positioned and bent to the inside, but moves straight on three tracks, usually along the side of the school, in perfect rhythm and with Schwung (often translated as impulsion, but also incorporating the springing, swinging movement of the hindquarters, back and legs of the horse). While the hindquarters move almost normally straight ahead, the fore-hand has been brought to the centre of the school to move at such a distance from the outside edge, through curving of the spine, so that the outside shoulder of the horse is in front of its inside hip and that the inside hind leg touches the ground in the direction of the outside front leg.

The purpose of the shoulder-in is to release the horse from the inside rein, to improve the contact of the outside rein and to prepare it ultimately for a primarily diagonal influence of the aids which has a collective effect.

Getting the horse to step up with increasing contact towards the outside rein, in connection with the raised requirements regarding the flexibility of the spine, results in distinct improvement of the correct head position and elevation. The degree of flexion of the hocks and the placing of the inside hind leg forwards under the centre of gravity, as well as the mobility of the front legs in the region of the shoulders – the freedom of the shoulders – are particularly promoted through this movement.

During shoulder-in, the horse, seen from the front, moves forwards on three tracks. The outside front leg and the inside hind leg touch the ground on the second track. Photograph: Bronkhorst

The shoulder-in cannot be compared to any other exercise – it has as little in common with crossing over as with the lateral movements. Instead it should be regarded as a connecting link between the relaxing and the collecting lateral movements. Its effect can be enhanced if it is performed on curved lines, for example, in the corners or on a circle.

During the crossing of the front legs, an almost normal straight movement of the hind legs, the horse, viewed from the front, moves on three tracks on which four legs are active. A correctly curved spine would not allow the forehand to move further in onto the fourth track and such a movement should be dismissed as faulty.

Prerequisites

Prerequisites for the rider

Theoretical foundations

- The rider has acquainted himself with theory of the requirements of the exercise, knows the significance of the outside rein, which determines the degree of the correct head position, and is able to correctly interpret the terms degree of bending and correct head position.

The seat

- The straight upper body, with its weight divided equally between each seat bone and the crotch, allows the rider the required independence from the stirrups that forms the prerequisite for placing both legs in the forward driving position. This is a hand's width behind the girth and prevents the hindquarters from falling out.
- The upper body has already achieved a certain stability in order to be able to react against possible resistance on the part of the horse. The lumbar region of the rider is mobile enough for him to be able to execute the positioning of the shoulder of the horse through the upper body.
- The rider has developed enough sensitivity in the seat to be able to distinguish between the stretching and bending phases of the hind legs.

Prerequisites for the horse

Physiological foundations

- The horse possesses a reasonably stable neck held in a bent position, which only needs to have a slight elevation and moderately positioned head to correspond with the moderate degree of bending of the head and lateral curvature of the spine.

On the aids

- The horse moves forwards at the rider's request, remains in front of the legs, and possesses relatively consolidated reactions and the necessary willingness to co-operate in order to be able to react correctly to the aids on both sides.
- Control of the poll, chewing on the bit and an active back have been achieved through relaxing exercises.

Execution

Preparatory exercises

In order to ensure that faults do not occur at the beginning of this movement, it is important to thoroughly prepare the horse beforehand with regard to correct head position, bending and elevation. Exercises such as riding with a slight inside bend and in particular the shoulder-fore as an exercise, which lies between riding with a slight inside bend and the shoulder-in, are a foundation for the correct build-up to the following shoulder-in.

Preparation for the movement

Although the exercise can in principle always be ridden on every line, its benefit will only be proven to its full extent on the outside edge of the school, because it is here that the hindquarters cannot fall out. Therefore, the best point from which to develop this movement is from out of the first corner of the long side of the school.

The focal point of the preparation is the correct riding of this corner. In the same way as in every turn, the rider shortens the inside rein before the corner, the horse's head is in the correct position and the horse is accepting and chewing on the bit. The rider raises the inside hand slightly to regulate the degree of bending. After the horse has been ridden through the corner, the rider ensures that the horse maintains this position of the head, in order to keep it for the entire length of the long side. It is sufficient if the rider can see the horse's eye and nostril in this position. The crest of the mane should tilt to the inside.

The inside leg retains gait and impulsion and drives the inside hind leg, which is lifting off towards the inside rein. At the same time, through its position on the girth, it prevents the horse from falling out over the inside shoulder into the centre of the school. Thus, it remains near the outside edge, which makes the work of the rider's outside calf, positioned in the counterpart position behind the girth, easier. The rider shifts his weight to the inside seat bone and thereby already encourages the flexion of the hocks and the placing of the horse's inside hind leg underneath the horse during the preparative phase. The horse is now bent evenly around the inside leg and has moved through the corner.

The aids

The rider's shoulders, which are already turned in the direction of the movement when riding through the corner, turn further in at the start of the long side to correspond with the degree of bending needed to lead the horse in towards the centre of the school.

The well-carried rider's hands follow the turn of the upper body and convey the aids to the horse until its outside shoulder is positioned in front of the inside hip. Thus the inside hand has a slightly lateral leading position and is raised higher in order to adapt to the degree of bending of the horse's head. It is thereby carried in front of, and higher than, the outside hand and is busy retaining the horse's contact (chewing) on the bit with effective half-halts and accelerating the horse's increased contact on the inside rein. The outside rein is carried close to the horse's neck. It determines the degree of the position of the head and maintains a steady elevation.

The horse is now positioned and bent correctly, has left the first track with its forehand and is moving on three tracks with its four legs, approximately as if it wanted to change the rein diagonally through the school.

In order to prevent this, the inside rein goes into action, the rider using half-halts to ensure that the horse cannot move forward any further towards the centre of the school. The horse is "called back" so-to-speak and the forehand is pushed outward towards the outside rein. The rider's inside leg on the girth also participates in this aid. It not only maintains the gait but also encourages the inside hind leg of the horse to move further forward so that the horse continues to bend its ribcage to the inside.

The horse, which is now trying to move back out, is held up in position by the outside rein and stabilised through half-halts. From now on it stays exactly in the centre between both reins with a perfect degree of bending and correct head position. The rein aids are repeated as described for the length of the long side whenever the horse attempts to leave this point.

The hindquarters are prevented from falling out by the outside leg, in its retaining position approximately one hand's width behind the girth, in conjunction with the outside edge of the school. The outside leg also participates in the forward driving aids which, in the course of further training, are gathered up increasingly by the outside rein and transformed into the elevation of the horse.

Conclusion of the movement

The shoulder-in finishes before reaching the second corner of the long side, approximately level with the point for the diagonal change of rein, and the forehand is moved back on track, in co-ordination with the hindquarters, by the rider's inside leg and rein. For this purpose, the rider straightens his shoulder axis, carries both hands back in their normal position, and drives the horse into the next corner with the inside leg.

Evaluation

The shoulder-in is a movement that is ridden in almost every dressage test at an advanced level. Whilst the dressage test evaluates the perfection with regard to impulsion, regularity, lateral bend and the regular work on three tracks, the main reason for riding this movement in daily schooling is the bending effect, even despite small imperfections in the course of the exercise. The degree to which the rider values this aim gives an idea as to whether he has understood the sense and purpose of the movement correctly and is able to translate it into action.

Critical moments

From the point of view of the horse, the difficulty of this exercise is certainly that owing to its lateral bend, it is forced to look and be driven in one direction in which it ultimately is not allowed to move. Particularly in the initial phase, in the region of the point of change at the beginning of the long side, the preparation of this movement could easily be taken for that which also forms the start of a number of other movements.

Horses that remember the diagonal and the extension of the trot, which is often combined with it, may occasionally increase their tempo and accelerate forwards so that even a very fast reacting rider will suddenly find himself on the second or third track.

If this occurs several times, the introduction of the exercise should at first simply be moved by a few metres past the point of change and can then be achieved smoothly by riding with a slight inside bend and the shoulder-fore.

Achievable degree of skill

If one views the shoulder-in as the forerunner of the lateral movements, these can be counted as the achievable degree of skill. However, as it is also strictly speaking a completely independent exercise, the actual increase of the skill level is in fact the more perfect completion of the elevation, correct head position, bending and collection.

Faults and corrections

The shoulder-in requires a high degree of sensitive feeling by the rider's hands regarding the correct working on the neck formation. Therefore riders who pull on the reins and a resisting horse will very easily produce faulty positions and twisting in the region of the poll and neck. In addition, damage to the cervical spine and pain in the area of the parotid gland can also lead to completely distorted positions of the head and neck.

Distortion in the poll

The term 'degree of bending' refers to the exact lateral alignment of the horse's head in relation to the positioned neck. Thus the arc of the positioned neck curves evenly from the withers to the forelock without a kink. In this position, the rear part of the horse's lower jaw tucks underneath the neck. The line of the nose down from the horse's forehead remains vertical. This state can only be attained if the horse willingly relaxes the upper part of the neck between the first and second cervical vertebrae, atlas and axis.

Many horses twist in the poll in order to achieve a more effective resistance against the inside rein. They do this by turning the nose outward and so take the inside part of the lower jaw outside the area of the inner side of the bridle. A crookedly held head with a stiff poll gives the impression that the rider is constantly pulling on the outside rein.

Correction of this is relatively easy, as the height of the rider's inside hand is responsible for the correct degree of bending, as well as the way it works. Initially, check if the length of the outside rein and the height of the outside hand allow the correct head position that is demanded by the inside rein. If this is the case, and the fault persists, the inside hand needs to be carried higher and must become more active. Instead of pulling or holding the rein immobile against the horse's mouth, the rider needs to perform half-halts which improve the horse's chewing on the bit. Only then can the rider start using his inside leg more actively.

Other horses become rigid in the poll area and turn their nose to the inside. Again the line from the forehead straight down the nose is no longer vertical. As a rule, this fault indicates that the rider's inside hand is carried high,

This horse twists in the poll area: the line from the forehead down the nose is turned outward.

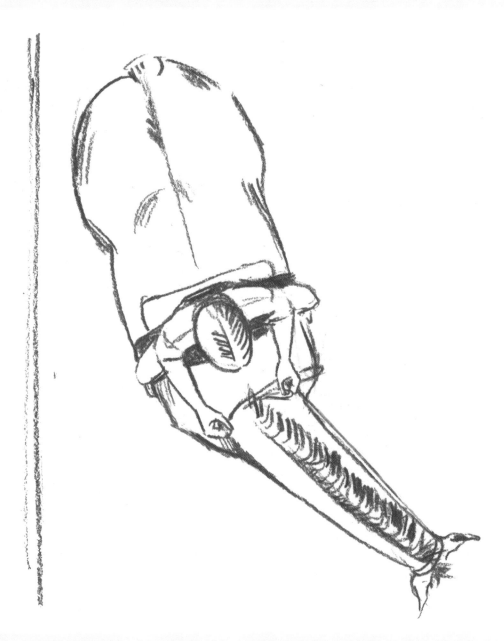

The neck of this horse is laterally over-bent and shows a distinct misalignment to the bending of the spine.

maybe too high, and is unable to relax the pressure in the mouth through suitable half-halts.

In order to remove the resistance, the inside hand needs to be carried lower and must become more active so that the horse comes down, chewing on the bit. The outside rein needs to be shortened. If this is still insufficient, the rider can lift his outside hand higher so that the outside hand is carried higher than the inside one until the fault is eliminated.

Distortion in the neck

A properly bent neck impresses through the even arc of the cervical spine, which is continued in the horse's head and back. This leads to the crest tilting to the inside.

Pulling on the inside rein, without any sensitivity, pulls the neck of willing horses, in particular, too far to the inside in such a way that the bend of the neck represents a gross misalignment to the bend of the spine. The horse is able to defend itself against this misalignment by distortion in the neck. There are as many opportunities for this as there are cervical vertebrae.

The classic form of distortion in the neck can be observed best from the front. While optically the correctly bent horse is between the rider's knees not just with its body but also with its head and neck, the over-bent horse, which is distorted in the neck, seems to need at least two tracks depending on the length of the neck. The horse moves on one track with its four legs, the neck hangs over the inside track and shows no bend or, in the worst-case scenario, even an opposing bend.

This is made possible through the so-called "breaking off" of the neck at the base, a kink in other words which can be observed clearly at the point where the neck rises out from between the shoulders. In this situation the horse's neck points to the centre of the school, not because of its even bend but due to the kink at the base of the neck. In this case the neck between the kink and the horse's head may not be bent at all or even bent to the outside.

It is easy to see that such a distortion of the neck is not simply a marring feature but that in the long term it can ultimately lead to significant damage to the entire skeleton of the horse.

This fault also has a significant effect on the rider. The propulsive force, which is developed by the horse's hind legs, if still in existence at all, now no longer exits at the lower jaw, where it could be transformed by the bit, but rather fizzles out at this kink – just like air from a hole in a defective tyre.

To correct this fault a radical rethink is required. The rider needs to use his legs actively. Initially, ensure that the outside rein does not work against the inside rein. Therefore it must be long enough not to impede the inside rein in ensuring the correct head position. The outside hand is carried as low as possible. The inside rein is raised but remains close to the horse's neck to reduce any lateral pulling effect. The inside hand becomes more active and promotes the horse accepting the bit by chewing, as well as the flexibility in the poll by performing numerous half-halts. The compulsion of distortion in the neck can be eliminated to the extent in which the half-halts coming through on the inner side allow the rider's inside leg to drive the horse forward and in which the horse strengthens the contact on the outside rein.

Falling-out through the shoulder

A falling-out through the shoulder can develop as a con-sequence of the distortion in the neck. Principally a horse can fall out through both shoulders. As a rule, the outside shoulder will be affected during the execution of exer-cises with incorrect head position. Every time the outside rein is not able to position and fix the neck from the base up, neck and head evade to the inside while the horse escapes to the outside over the insufficiently controlled shoulder. The result is a failure to bend the spine and the desired direction of the entire forehand into the centre of the school.

The correction of this fault is as obvious as its cause: because only the outside rein, in combination with an out-side leg, not positioned too far back, is capable of stabilis-ing the shoulder on the same side, and thereby eliminat-ing the fault. The horse needs to step up to and also establish contact with this rein. If the outside rein was the correct length, so that the horse was able to establish con-tact, and if all other faults described can be ruled out, it is the inside rein and leg that has not yet attained the desired goal of the movement.

More effective half-halts, which have an effect on the horse's mouth and allow the rider's inside leg to work prop-erly, will ensure that over time the horse will start loosening its contact with the inside rein and strengthen its contact with the outside rein. With increasing dominance the out-side rein is able to control the outside shoulder more and more effectively.

At the same time, the rider places his outside leg for-ward closer to the girth because its effect as a retaining aid is not required anyway, owing to the lack of bending of the horse. Close to the girth, it ensures that the drifting outside shoulder is checked and driven in the direction of the horse's head. It also diverts the movement of the hind legs to the horse's mouth, until it arrives at the outside rein and the horse is once more straightened in itself.

To begin with, the growing efforts of the horse proper-ly corrected in this way to move into the centre of the school needs to be restrained by both reins, with only the essential careful handling. Half-halts that are too harsh would soon kill off the courage of a horse to perform this distinct forward moving tendency. They would trap the horse between the hands and legs and cause it to return to its old faults or to adopt others. Riders, who have recog-nised this correctly, and try to remedy it with an active outside leg, will conclude the movement on the second or third track. Ultimately, it is only a matter of time before the half-halts get through in such a way that they can balance out the effects of active legs, and the horse remains on the first track.

While such riders will be successful after a short period of time, riders who do not correct their horses which 'stick' to the edge of the school are doomed to failure because the faults will reinforce themselves and will in future run like a thread through all further training projects.

This horse is bent excessively and distorted in the neck. This results in the fall-out over the shoulder.

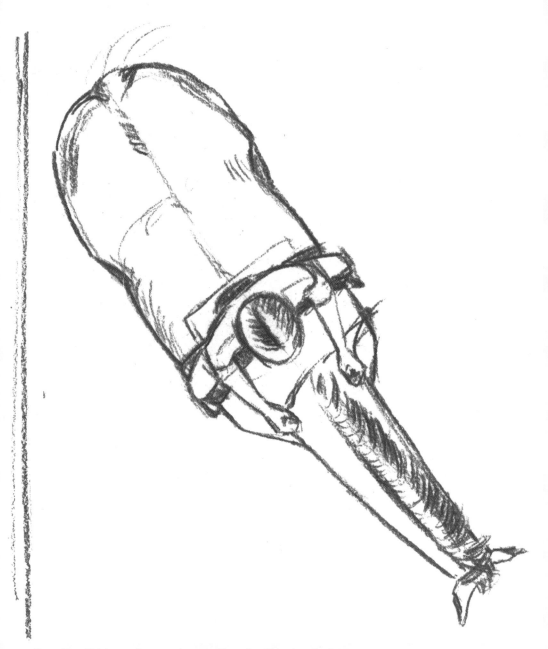

The spine of this horse shows no degree of bending. Therefore the horse moves on four tracks and not as desired on three.

Lack of bending

As described, the hindquarters move straight ahead, almost normally if the movement is executed correctly and at an advanced level. At the same time, the forehand is turned into the centre of the school and the inside hind leg follows in the track of the outside front leg, on the second of the three tracks. These specifications can only be achieved via a pronounced bending of the horse's spine. One of the most important training goals of this movement is to improve this bending of the spine.

Even an amateur will immediately recognise a horse that lacks bend through the spine. This is due to the fact that the hind legs of the horse need to cross over. As soon as the forehand is turned into the centre of the school, the hindquarters of a horse with a rigid and stiff back also, necessarily, turn in towards the centre of the school. The aid of the outside edge of the school is no longer effective because it no longer runs parallel to the outside hind leg, but instead behind it almost crosswise in relation to the tail. If the rider's inside leg is unable to create a hollow in the ribcage of the horse, and if the outside retaining leg behind the girth does not stop the horse's outside hind leg from falling-out at the same time, the inside hind leg of the horse will no longer step under the horse's centre of gravity. Instead it will move predominantly sideways as in leg yielding.

If, in this case, hard-boiled riders bend their horses towards the centre of the school to such an extent that at a cursory glance it looks like a certain degree of shoulder-in, these horses will consequently move forward on four tracks. At this point even an inexperienced judge will observe this cheating and punish it with a respectively low score, because such demonstrations completely lack the essential characteristics of the movement.

Therefore, it is important during daily training to test not only theoretical knowledge of the rider with regard to the objective of this movement, but also to fall back on corrective exercises that will effect an improved flexibility of the horse's back.

The means to do so are limited by nature, because horses at this level of training are as a rule those that are at the beginning of their career. All turns, from the circle to the volte to serpentines through the whole of the school, are suitable exercises to supple up a horse's back.

In order to be able to make use of the rider's inside leg, which is responsible to a high degree for the bending of the ribcage, more effective exercises, such as crossing over the inside leg on the open side of a circle (leg yielding) and frequent transitions to the canter from this movement, are exactly right.

Remarks

In the hands of an expert, the shoulder-in is one of the best means to eliminate entrenched faults. The bending effect of the movement is as essential for the stiff side (for most horses the left side) as the straightening effect is for the difficult right side.

This bending effect, however, requires an intact horse's back. Damage to the spine, such as 'Kissing Spines' and similar defects, mean that execution of the bending requested by this movement is painful for the horse and this leads to resistance. Therefore, such defects need to be excluded with certainty before trying to enforce corrective measures otherwise this exercise, due to its high degree of effectiveness, would cause more harm than good.

2. Travers

When executed correctly, the observer will see a horse with good elevation that moves forwards with its front and hindquarters on two tracks, positioned and bent in the direction it is moving, along the side of the school. While the forehand moves on the first track, the hindquarters are off-set towards the centre of the school to such a degree that the front and hind legs cross over on four track lines.

The purpose of the travers is to improve the pliability of the inner side, the relaxation of the inside rein and the Durchlässigkeit (suppleness) of the rider's outside leg, which drives the horse sideways. In addition, it trains the eye of the rider who, through the optical guidance of the outside edge of the school, will get a feel for the correct positioning of the horse at the correct angle much faster than on other lines.

Asking the horse to step up to the inside rein in connection with the growing demand for flexibility of the spine, results in distinct improvements to the degree of bending, correct head position, elevation and the freedom of the shoulder. In particular, this movement promotes the flexion of the hocks and the placing of the inside hind legs forwards under the centre of gravity, as well as the mobility of the hindquarters in the area of the hips and flanks.

During the travers (also known as haunches in) the horse is positioned and bent in the direction in which it is moving forwards. Front and hind legs cross over on four tracks.
Photograph: Bronkhorst

The travers is a collecting lateral movement which is ridden exclusively along the long outside edge of the school. While the outside edge of the school guides the hindquarters during the shoulder-in, and thereby relieves the retaining riders' outside leg, the forehand is guided during the travers and the outside rein is relieved. Thereby the movement is the exact opposite of the shoulder-in, with opposing definitions of tasks.

The more perfect the lateral bend, the less the front legs cross over. In the case of a fully trained horse, the front legs barely cross over at all. It is only because the horse's front legs are not at the front of the lateral bend, because of the protruding neck and head, that the forehand is prevented from moving almost wholly straight ahead similar to the movement of the hindquarters during the shoulder-in.

Prerequisites

Prerequisites for the rider

Theoretical foundations

- The rider has acquainted himself with the theory of the exercise. He knows the significance of the outside retaining leg and is able to correctly interpret the terms degree of bending and correct head position.

The seat

- The straight upper body, with its weight divided equally between each seat bone and the crotch, allows the rider the required independence from the stirrups which forms the prerequisite for the placing of both legs in any position that drives the horse forward or has a retaining effect.
- The upper body has already achieved a certain stability in order to be able to react against possible resistance on the part of the horse.
- In the lumbar region, the rider is mobile enough to be able to adapt the axis of his hips and shoulders to those of the horse.
- The rider has developed enough sensitivity in the seat to be able to distinguish between the stretching and flexing phases of the hind legs.

Prerequisites for the horse

Physiological foundations

- The horse possesses a steady neck which only needs to be positioned initially in a slight elevation in order to correspond with the positioning of the head and the slight curvature of the spine.

On the aids

- The horse moves forwards at the rider's request, remains in front of the legs and possesses relatively well-established reactions and the necessary willingness to co-operate, in order to be able to react correctly to the forward driving and lateral aids.
- Control of the neck and poll, chewing on the bit and an active back have been achieved through relaxing exercises.

Execution

Preparatory exercises

A thorough preparation of the horse with regard to correct head position, bending and elevation is indispensable for the travers. Exercises such as riding with a slight inside bend and, in particular, the shoulder-fore (situated between riding with a slight inside bend and the shoulder-in) form the foundation for the correct execution of the travers.

Preparation for the movement

Although the lateral movement should be ridden on any line as a half-pass or half-pass lateral movement, its full use in the form of the travers only comes into effect with the support of the outside edge of the school, because here the forehand cannot evade to the outside. For this reason, it is best to develop the travers from the first corner of the long side of the school.

Therefore, the focal point of the preparation lies in the correct riding of this corner. As before any turn, the rider shortens the inside rein before the corner, positions the horse and makes sure it is chewing on the bit. The inside hand is raised slightly in order to regulate the head position. After the corner has been negotiated, the rider continues in this position in order to maintain it for the entire length of the long side of the school. It is sufficient if he can see the horse's eye and nostril in this position. The crest of the mane tilts to the inside.

The rider's inside leg retains gait and impulsion and once more drives the horse deeply into the corner. At the same time, in its position forward on the girth, it prevents the horse falling into the centre of the school via its inside shoulder. Thus, the horse remains near the outer edge of the school with its forehand. This facilitates the work of the rider's outside leg in the retaining position behind the girth.

The rider shifts his weight onto the inside seat bone and this promotes the flexion of the hocks and the placing of the inside hind leg forwards under the centre of gravity during preparation. The horse is now positioned in the direction of movement, is bent evenly around the rider's inside leg and has passed the apex of the corner.

The aids

Before the hindquarters, following the forehand around the corner, can reach the outside edge of the school with its first track, they are restrained by the rider's outside laterally driving leg and kept on the second track. Thereby, the correct head position, bending and direction of the horse's barrel that was formed in the corner are kept unchanged and retained over the entire length of the long side of the school. The four legs remain on four track lines and now begin to cross over, whereby each outside leg crosses in front and over the inside leg. This results in the lateral movement of the horse.

The rider's inside leg, still in the front on the girth, drives the horse towards the outside edge of the school, and the inside rein. The inside rein calls the rushing horse to order by means of energetic half-halts. At the same time, it limits the lateral scope of motion of the horse's inside hind leg to such an extent that the hindquarters do not point into the centre of the school too steeply, and the outside hind leg is able to continue to cross over rhythmically.

The hindquarters of the horse are only brought in towards the centre of the school at an angle to the track that does not exceed 45 degrees. Thereby, the lateral scope of motion of forehand and hindquarters remain the same. Photograph: Horses in Media/Lenz

The rider's outside leg lies just behind the girth. It contributes to the forward-driving aids and prevents the outside shoulder from falling out, as far as this is permitted by the predominantly lateral driving effect. This drives the outside hind leg forwards and over the inside hind leg over the entire length of the long side of the school. For the success of the exercise, it is of utmost importance to find the correct position for this leg from where it can do both jobs equally well.

The inside rein needs to process the motion transferred to it through the outside edge of the school, which both of the rider's legs drive it towards continuously. This inside rein pressure, which the horse feels in its mouth, is processed through suitable half-halts. They ensure that very soon the horse chews responsively on the inside rein and relinquishes its contact.

This basically fulfils the core purpose of the travers movement. Now the outside rein, which retains the correct position, can take up the horse. Over time this rein will increasingly take over the work of the outside edge of the school and is thus even more suitable to affect an elevation of the horse's neck, and to fix it at the base.

Now the aids need to be attuned to each other in such a way that the lateral scope of motion of the forehand and hindquarters remains the same. As a result the horse, once it is bent and positioned correctly, does not change its shape over the entire length of the long side of the school. In other words, that it remains centrally between the aids. Only after the horse remains stable between hands and legs at all times can the rider attempt to ride this exercise at an increased tempo to heighten expression and dynamics.

Conclusion of the movement

Before reaching the second corner of the long side of the school, and to conclude the exercise, the horse is driven forwards with both the rider's legs to bring it back onto the first track, in the same way as when concluding a volte.

Evaluation

The travers is an exercise that is unfortunately only demanded very rarely in dressage tests. Whereas in a test, its perfect execution with regard to impulsion, regularity, lateral bend and the even work on four tracks is evaluated, the forward-driving measures and the bending are the more important effects to strive for during daily training, irrespective of possible small signs of unevenness in the course of the exercise. The attention that the rider affords to these details shows whether he has understood the sense and purpose of the exercise correctly and is able to translate it into action.

Critical moments

Generally you will find that critical moments usually only occur in the initial phase of the exercise, when the rider's outside leg reacts too late or does not have any effect after riding through the corner. Then the horse, following its natural pattern of movement, will attempt to move its hindquarters onto the first track as well.

Pushing the hindquarters in towards the centre of the school after they have reached the first track, so that the horse gives the impression of a veering car, is incorrect equitation and technically false. It is easier and more correct to regain the initial position that riding a corner offers by riding a volte in order to intercept the hindquarters anew on the second track, just before the conclusion of the volte. This new build-up is also recommended if difficulties occur in the course of the length of the long side, for example if impulsion, regularity or lateral bend have been lost.

Achievable degree of skill

If the build-up has been correct, the travers can be regarded as the first true lateral movement. Thereby, the achievable degree of skill does not only include a perfect completion of the exercise but as a rule leads directly to half-pass and half-pass lateral movements.

Faults and corrections

The travers places high demands on the influence of the rider's inside hand with respect to the correct translation of the impulsion coming from behind into the elevation and correct position of the neck. Therefore, riders who pull on the reins, and horses that resist, will very easily produce faulty positions and twisting in the region of the

A rider who pulls on the inside rein will lead to the horse over-bending and twisting in the neck.

poll and neck. In addition to damage to the cervical spine and pain in the area of the parotid gland, this can also lead to completely distorted positions of the head and neck.

The faults described in the preceding chapter concerning the shoulder-in, such as the distortion in the poll and in the neck, as well as the neck that kinks at the base, can also often be observed during the execution of the travers.

This exercise requires very well-tuned legwork on the part of the rider. Both legs have to fulfil clearly defined tasks and inaccuracy can have a significant negative effect on the successful execution of the exercise.

Lack of bending

As described, the forehand and hindquarters move on two tracks if the movement is executed correctly, while the four legs cross over on four track lines. In contrast to the shoulder-in, these specifications cannot only be achieved through a pronounced bending of the horse's spine, which is one of the most important training goals of this movement, but also with rigidly stiff horses without any curvature of the ribcage at all.

In particular, a horse that produces a kink in his neck while lacking any kind of bending can fool the amateur, while the expert recognises this immediately as the horse needs to cross over just as intensively with his forelegs as with his hind legs. In the case of a horse with a non-yielding, rigid back,

this is due to the forehand also twisting inwards as soon as the hindquarters are positioned towards the centre of the school on the second track. Owing to the fact that now the forehand and hindquarters are both positioned at the exact same angle in relation to the outside edge of the school, all four legs need to cross over to the same degree.

The leading effect of the outside edge of the school also no longer applies, because it now no longer runs parallel to the horse's jaw, but instead in front of it, almost straight across the forehead. If the rider's inside leg is unable to create a hollow in the ribcage section of the horse, and if the outside retaining leg behind the girth does not stop the horse's outside hind leg from falling out, the inside hind leg of the horse will no longer step under the horse's centre of gravity. Instead, it will move predominantly sideways just as in leg yielding.

If these horses are then also positioned far enough towards the centre of the school by hard-boiled riders that, at a cursory glance, it looks a bit like a travers, they give the impression that they are constantly running against the outside edge of the school. In order to prevent this, they develop angular-looking evasive actions with the forehand pretty much resembling the wooden swaying steps of an untalented dancer. At this point even an inexperienced judge will necessarily observe this cheating and punish it with a respectively low score, because such demonstrations completely lack the essential characteristics of the movement.

Therefore, not only does the rider's theoretical knowledge, with regard to the goal of this exercise, need to be checked during daily training but he also needs to fall back on corrective exercises which will effect an improved pliability of the horse's back.

The means are limited by nature because horses at this level of training are, as a rule, those that are at the beginning of their career. All turns from the circle, from the volte to serpentines through the whole of the school, are suitable exercises to supple up a horse's back.

In order for the rider to be able to use his inside leg, which is largely responsible for the bending of the ribcage, more effectively in the future, exercises such as crossing over the inside leg on the open side of a circle (leg yielding) and frequent transitions to the canter following on from this exercise are exactly right.

Remarks

The closeness of the outside edge of the school significantly increases the risk of injury if the horse is given incorrect aids. Scratches to the head and injuries to the coronet bands, which the horses strike during crossing over, can occur. Over-stretching of the ligaments of the front legs can also often be observed. Hindquarters, forced too far into the centre of the school, force the horse to straddle its hind legs wide apart which can cause painful strains of the muscles and damage to the lumbar spine.

Care should be taken when executing the travers. During the cold season, in particular, the rider needs to ensure that before attempting the travers the horse's muscles have been warmed up and are sufficiently supple through relaxing exercises.

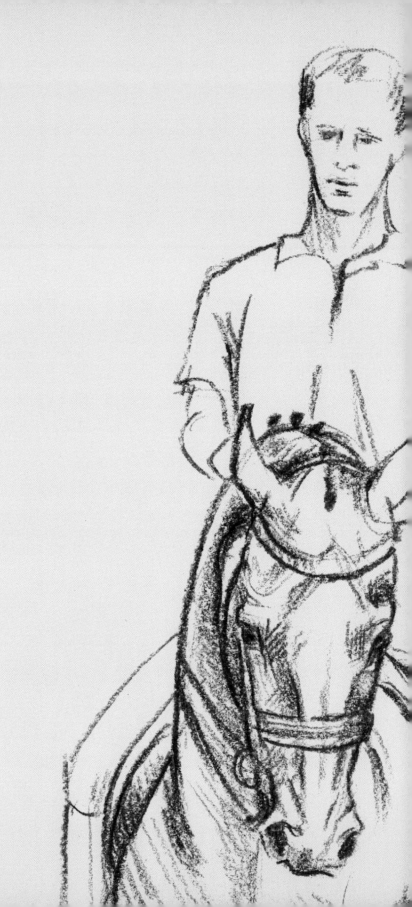

3. Renvers

When executed correctly the observer will see a horse with a good elevation that is positioned and bent in the direction it is moving forwards in, and moves along the side of the school with its front and hindquarters moving on two tracks. While the hindquarters move on the first track the forehand is set-off towards the centre of the school to such a degree that the front and hind legs cross over on four track lines.

The renvers leads the horse to the aids in a predominantly diagonal, collective way but in particular also reinforces the contact with, and the Durchlässigkeit (suppleness) of, the outside rein. Asking the horse to step up to the inside rein in connection with the increasing demand for flexibility of the spine, results in distinct improvements to the degree of bending, correct head position, and elevation. This movement promotes the flexion of the hocks, in particular, and the placing of the inside hind legs forwards under the centre of gravity, as well as the mobility of the hindquarters in the area of the hips and flanks.

The renvers is a lateral movement of collection that is ridden exclusively along the long outside edge of the school. While, during the shoulder-in, the hindquarters of

During the renvers the front and hind legs of the horse cross over on four tracks. In this case the forehand moves on the second track, the hindquarters on the first track. Photograph: Bronkhorst

the horse are retained on the side by the outside edge of the school, they are, at most, still led by it during the renvers. Unfortunately the renvers is demanded only very rarely in dressage tests.

The exercise is a difficult one because the lateral bend and direction of movement of the horse need to be changed around completely in a very short span of time, right at the start of the initial phase.

Prerequisites

Prerequisites for the rider

Theoretical foundations

- The rider has acquainted himself with the theory of the requirements of the exercise. He knows the significance of the outside leg in its different positions.
- He is able to correctly interpret the terms degree of bending and correct head position.

The seat

- The straight upper body, with its weight divided equally between each seat bone and the crotch, allows the rider the required independence from the stirrups which forms the prerequisite for the placing of both legs in any position which drives the horse forward or has a retaining effect.
- The upper body has already achieved a certain stability in order to be able to react against possible resistance on both reins.

- In the lumbar region, the rider is mobile enough to be able to adapt the axis of his hips and shoulders to those of the horse.
- The rider has developed sensitivity in the seat to the point where he is able to distinguish between the stretching and flexing phases of the hind legs.

Prerequisites for the horse

Physiological foundations

- The horse possesses a steady neck at the base which only needs to be slightly positioned in a good elevation in order to correspond with the matching positioning of the head and the slight curvature of the spine.

On the aids

- The horse accepts the forward-driving aids and remains steadily in front of the rider's legs.
- The horse possesses relatively well-established reactions and the necessary willingness to co-operate in order to be able to react correctly to the forward driving and lateral aids as well as to the retaining effects of the reins.
- Control of the neck and poll, chewing on the bit and an active back have been achieved through relaxing exercises.

Execution

Preparatory exercises

A correctly executed renvers is achieved, essentially, through the fast, sensitive introduction at the start of the long side of the school. Here, the horse needs to be re-positioned completely within a space of only a few metres. Exercises such as serpentines through the entire school, shallow loops down the length of the long side and frequent changes of rein through a circle promote the willingness and relaxation of the horse to let the rider position and bend it quickly in a new direction. In the case of well-trained horses, lateral half-pass movements and half-pass which are combined with frequent changes of direction can improve the suppleness of the spine and impart to the rider the necessary sensitive action of his hands.

Preparation for the movement

As mentioned already, the lateral movement renvers is executed exclusively on the outside edge of the school and has to be developed out of the first corner of the long side of the school. Therefore, the focal point of the prepa-ration lies in the correct riding of this corner: the horse is positioned in the direction of movement and encouraged to chew on the bit. The rider's inside leg maintains the gait and once more drives the horse deep into the corner.

The rider's shoulders, which are already turned in the direction of the movement in the corner, are now turned significantly further to the inside as far as necessary in order to lead the forehand of the horse in towards the centre of the school. This is done as if the rider intended to change reins diagonally across half of the school. The rider's well-carried hands follow the turn of the upper body and pass on the aids to the horse. The horse consequently moves towards the diagonal in the arc of a quarter of a volte. Dur-ing this, the inside hand is positioned in a slightly lateral lead-ing position and remains raised in order to adapt the posi-tion of the head to the increasing bending. Thereby it is held in front of and over the outside hand and has the task of ensuring that the horse remains chewing on the bit and establishing the horse's increased contact on the inside rein. The outside rein close to the neck limits the correct head position and ensures the steady elevation. The rider's outside leg, in its retaining position, has little to do so far because the closeness to the outside edge of the school can essentially prevent a fall-out of the hindquarters.

The horse is now positioned and bent to the inside and has left the first track with its forehand. The hindquarters, however, are still aligned almost parallel to the outside rail of the school. If the rider were to give on the inside rein and not do anything further, the horse would change rein diag-onally across half the school.

In order to prevent this, the horse is asked, with suitable impulses on the outside rein, to position itself into the new direction of movement on the second track fluently and with a pure degree of bending and correct head position; in other words without distortion in the neck. It is sufficient if the rider can see the horse's eye and nostril in this position. The rider shortens this rein and holds his hand higher thus making it the new inside rein. The position of the head is fixed, the crest tilts in the new direction of movement. The rider has lengthened the new outside rein in order not to hamper the re-positioning. He shifts his weight smoothly and gradually onto the new inside seat bone without disturbing the horse.

The horse is now positioned in the new direction of movement and its head and neck are on the second track at the start of the long side of the school. Its four legs move on four track lines. Owing to the re-positioning of the neck, which has also influenced the line of the horse's back, the hindquarters are no longer aligned parallel to the outside edge of the school – the outside edge of the school now runs instead at an angle to the point of the hip. In this position, the hindquarters are fixed by the rider's new outside leg and prevented from falling out. Thus, the horse is positioned at an optimum to the line. The correct starting position has been achieved and the preparations are concluded.

The aids

The rider initiates the renvers by using the outside retaining leg to actively prevent the hindquarters leaving the first track. The hindquarters are thereby kept next to the outside edge of the school, where they need to remain during the entire course of the movement. This guarantees an even, steady alignment of the barrel of the horse to the line of the second track. The rider's outside leg has become a laterally acting one and during the exercise drives the horse's corresponding outside hind leg forwards and over the inside hind leg during the phase of suspension. The leg pushes the horse along the line in close co-operation with the outside rein, which limits the correct head position and pushes the forehand in the direction of movement.

The four legs on their four track lines now move forwards and sideways as in all lateral movements. During the renvers, the task of the inside rein is simply to restrain a horse that has become too fast, and to return it to the rider's legs, through fast effective half-halts. Apart from that, it is only responsible for maintaining the correct head position and degree of bending so that it does not become an unpredictable opponent of the outside rein.

With his weight shifted to the inside and his inside leg in the forward-driving position on the girth, the rider ensures the necessary motion forwards. This in turn is retained by the outside rein and directed into the desired direction of movement. The horse collects itself between the rider's inside leg and the outside rein, the movements become more upright.

Both reins jointly prevent the horse leaving the imaginary line along the second track, while the rider's outside leg ensures the necessary lateral tendency and at the same time prevents the hindquarters from twisting or falling out.

These aids, which need to adapt to the changing conditions during the execution of the renvers, can only function correctly if the rider has learnt to be variable enough with his aids and not to lose sight of the imaginary line the horse is meant to move along.

Conclusion of the movement

The renvers is concluded before the end of the long side, no later than at the last marker of the long side of the school, by positioning the forehand in alignment with the hindquarters. The rider takes his outside leg from its laterally driving position back to the front on the girth and leads the forehand to the outside edge of the school, in front of the hindquarters, with the help of the outside rein, which limits the degree of bending. The inside rein is lengthened and thus becomes the outside rein again. Now the horse moves with all its legs on the track and is bent to the inside in order to move correctly through the second corner of the long side of the school.

Evaluation

The expert observer will learn from the renvers how far the fine-tuning co-operation between horse and rider has come and how far the rider has developed a feeling for rhythm. The trainer should in particular evaluate the influence of the outside rein, which has to perform the main task of the exercise.

Critical moments

The critical moment of this exercise occurs right at the beginning, when the horse needs to be positioned and bent completely around the other way between the first and second track. In the broadest sense, the introduction is similar to the introduction of a shallow loop. Very difficult horses can be made to half-pass on this line before developing the renvers.

The unaccustomed direction of vision towards the centre of the school can also initially confuse inexperienced riders in particular. Once these riders have realised that irrespective of the name of the lateral movement and the line

of direction, it is only important to align a horse correctly to the line and ride along this, the renvers is much easier to understand.

Achievable degree of skill

The renvers ridden along the outside rail of the school is a completely independent exercise which, from a technical point of view and in comparison to other lateral movements, needs to be ridden along a special line. The achievable degree of skill is therefore a more perfect execution, which exhibits even more positioning, bending and scope of motion.

Faults and corrections

Faults such as the distortion in the poll and the neck, as well as all the faults listed under half-pass, can also be seen during the execution of the renvers.

Falling-out through the inside shoulder

Horses that are positioned in the direction of movement can be induced very easily to lean on the inside rein because they are moving towards it. In order to make this more substantial, they throw themselves over the inside shoulder in the direction of movement and at the same time drift sideways faster and faster, until the front legs move more laterally than the hind legs. The increasing

As in other movements, care should be taken when performing the renvers that the shoulder leads at all times and that the hindquarters do not lead as illustrated in this drawing.

pressure on the inside rein means that the rider can no longer drive the horse forwards, which intensifies the fault even more. The horse is no longer straight in itself, the rider can no longer stay on the line, and the horse falls back on the first track with the forehand due to the loss of the lateral bend.

To begin with, the rider needs to improve the Durchlässigkeit (suppleness) on the inside rein, which is responsible for the correct head position. Half-halts push the horse back against the rider's legs, raise the neck and lead it back in front of the direction of movement to ensure that the horse is straight within itself once more.

This horse falls out through the inside shoulder and shows none of the
necessary lateral bend. The forehand pushes back onto the first track.

Only then can the rider's inside leg support this aid. Close to the front, on the girth, it presses the shoulder, which is pushing away sideways behind the positioned neck, and drives the inside hind leg forwards to take up the weight under the centre of gravity. The ribcage on the same side contracts and the horse bends correctly if the co-operation with the outside retaining leg (lying a hand's width behind the girth to prevent a falling out of the hindquarters) functions properly. Very soon, a horse corrected in this manner will lessen the contact with the inside rein and will carry itself and accept the outside rein again. The fact that it moves away from the outside edge of the school and the rider finds himself on the third or fourth track at the end of the long side of the school simply proves consequent good correction and won't worry the expert in the slightest.

Remarks

The complicated introduction of this exercise means that many horses move too far into the centre of the school, particularly in the initial phase. Heavy-handed riders will often try to change this with strong hand actions. With time, shy horses will no longer dare to move far enough from the first track and will rub against the outside edge of the school with their hocks. Initially this will lead only to slight abrasions but after a short time it can end with capped hocks. Such an injury not only impairs the flexing action of the hocks but also looks ugly and can significantly lower the worth of a horse.

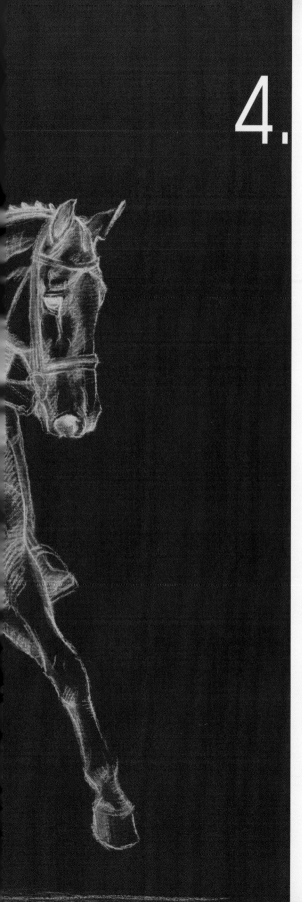

4. Half-pass, lateral half-pass movements

If executed correctly, the observer will see a horse with a good elevation that is positioned and bent in the direction in which it is moving and moves along in good rhythm on two tracks along a fixed line. The forehand leads slightly on this line, the hindquarters are turned inwards towards the centre of the school to such an extent that the front and hind legs cross over in an even flow of movement on four track lines.

The purpose of the half-pass is to lead the horse to a higher degree of collection and further improve the flexibility of neck and back by means of predominantly diagonally acting aids. Asking the horse to step up increasingly to the inside rein in connection with the rising demand for flexibility of the spine results in distinct improvements to the degree of bending, correct head position and elevation. The increasingly strengthened muscles of the haunches and the mobility of the hindquarters in the area of the hips and flanks promote the elevation of the movements and make the horse supple.

As with all lateral movements, half-pass is exclusively of a collective nature. In contrast to the lateral half-pass movements that can be ridden on your own chosen lines,

During the half-pass, the horse is positioned and bent in the direction of movement. The forehand leads, enabling the front and hind legs to cross over parallel in an even flow of motion. Photograph: Bronkhorst

the half-pass has to be performed on internationally uniformly defined tracks.

In competitions, tests can demand half, double half, full and double full as well as zigzag half-pass. A certain number of metres (quarter line) is determined for half-pass at the trot, a certain number of strides or metres at the canter for half-pass. The formerly customary half double and full double half-pass is these days no longer performed.

Lateral half-pass movements on track, chosen at will by the ride, are occasionally to be found in freestyle competition at shows, but in particular during daily training, and can improve the influence on the horse significantly, if the correct lines are chosen. Lateral half-pass movements, for example, can be ridden very well on circles or other curved lines in order to make use of the additional effect of the curved line. This places extremely high demands on the horse regarding the freedom of the shoulder, because in contrast to straight lines, where horses can be left in peace once they have been positioned correctly, the forehand on curved lines needs to be encouraged to lead the hindquarters continuously in order to be able to follow the constant bending. The front legs need to cross over to a much higher degree. However, this is precisely the training value of this exercise.

Prerequisites

Prerequisites for the rider

Theoretical foundations

- The rider has acquainted himself with the theoretical requirements of the exercise. He knows the significance of the diagonal aids and is able to correctly interpret the terms degree of bending and correct head position.

The seat

- The straight upper body, with its weight divided equally between each seat bone and the crotch, allows the rider the required independence from the stirrups that forms the prerequisite for the placing of both legs in any position which drives the horse forward or has a retaining effect.
- The upper body has already achieved a certain stability in order to be able to react against possible resistance on both reins.
- In the lumbar region the rider is mobile enough to be able to adapt the axis of his hips and shoulders to those of the horse.
- The rider has developed sensitivity in the seat to the point where he is able to distinguish between the stretching and flexing phases of the hind legs.

Prerequisites for the horse

Physiological foundations

- For this exercise it is essential that the horse possesses a neck steady at the base and set in an elevated to very elevated position, depending on its state of training, in combination with free shoulders which allow a light-footed crossing over of the front legs.

- Muscles and flexion of the hindquarters need to be trained well enough to guarantee dynamic action under the centre of gravity, even in a small space.

On the aids
- The horse is able to feel very light aids and follow these without delay.
- The horse possesses well-developed collection, and tight turns no longer pose a problem.
- The horse thinks and co-operates with the rider, is more or less fully balanced and is therefore able to change the direction of movement without any delay.

Execution

Preparatory exercises

Half-pass and lateral half-pass movements are the result of bending work during the shoulder-in and travers, led on the outer edge of the school, which will now be developed on one or several diagonal lines.

Preparation for the movement

Most half-passes are developed out of the first corner of the long side or start on the check points D or G of the centre line. Occasionally, they are demanded at the end of a volte in the middle of the long side of the school, and are therefore assigned to the lateral half-pass movements.

Therefore, the focal point of the preparation lies in the correct riding of these turns and corners. Before each turn, the rider shortens the inside rein before the corner, positions the horse and makes sure it is chewing on the bit. The inside hand is raised slightly, in order to regulate the position of the head. It is sufficient if the rider can see the horse's eye and nostril in this position. The crest tilts to the inside. After the corner has been executed, the rider continues to maintain this position of the head for the following half-pass.

The rider's inside leg retains gait and impulsion and drives the horse's inside hind leg, which is lifting off the ground towards the inside rein. At the same time, in its position up forward on the girth, it prevents the horse from falling towards the centre of the school via its inside shoulder. Thus the horse remains near the outer edge of the school with its forehand. This facilitates the work of the rider's outside leg in the retaining position behind the girth.

The rider shifts his weight onto the inside seat bone and thus promotes the flexion of the hocks and active striding forwards of the inside hind leg on the same side during the preparation stage. The horse is bent evenly around the rider's inside leg, has passed the apex of the corner and is close to the first marker of the long side.

If the rider now wanted to ride around the outside edge of the school, he would only have to give on the inside rein to enable the horse to move straight forwards. However, as he wants to half-pass on a line running diagonally through the school, he needs to position the shoulders of his horse further forwards.

To achieve this, he turns his shoulders further into the centre of the school as if he wanted to change the rein diagonally through the entire or half of the school. Well-carried hands follow the turn of the upper body and pass on the instructions to the horse, which consequently turns into the arc of a quarter volte on the diagonal. This means that the inside hand has a slightly lateral leading position and is raised higher in order to adapt to the position of the horse's head. It therefore is carried in front of and higher than the outside hand and is busy retaining the horse's contact (chewing) on the bit by means of effective half-halts and establishing the horse's increased contact on the inside rein. The outside rein, close to the horse's neck, determines the correct degree of bend and maintains a steady elevation. So far, the outside leg, in its retaining position, does not have much to do, because the closeness to the outside edge of the school can still prevent the hindquarters from falling out.

At this point, the horse, positioned and bent, has left the first track with its forehand. Its head and neck are already on the beginning of the diagonal and its four legs are on the four track lines. The hindquarters are aligned almost parallel to the outside edge of the school. Thereby, the horse is in an optimum position to now follow the line, the correct starting position has been achieved, and the preparations are concluded.

The aids

The rider initiates the half-pass by activating the outside retaining leg and preventing the hindquarters from stepping on the diagonal line. In this way they are kept on a second track on which they have to remain during the entire half-pass, and thus enable an unchanging alignment of the horse to the desired path. The outside leg, which has now become a laterally driving one because of its activities, drives the horse's outside hind leg forwards and over the inside leg, in its phase of suspension. The close co-operation with the outside rein, which limits the correct head position and pushes the forehand in the direction of movement, pushes the horse along the line.

Now the four legs on their four track lines move forwards and sideways, the horse is moving at a half-pass. During the course of the half-pass, the inside rein simply restrains a horse if it has become too hurried and returns it back to the rider's legs through fast, effective half-halts. Otherwise it is only responsible for maintaining the correct head position and degree of bending so that it does not become an unpredictable opponent of the outside rein.

The rider, with his weight still shifted to the inside and with his inside leg in the forward-driving position on the girth, ensures the necessary motion forwards, which in turn is retained by the outside rein and directed into the desired direction of movement. The horse collects itself between the rider's inside leg and the outside rein, the movements becoming more elevated.

Both reins jointly prevent the horse from crossing over the line it has to follow, while the rider's outside leg provides the

The rider, shifting his weight to the inside, induces the horse to step in front of and over the inside hind leg, with the outside hind leg under its centre of gravity. Photograph: Horses in Media/Streitpferd

necessary lateral movement and prevents the hindquarters from twisting or falling out.

These aids, which need to adapt to the constantly changing conditions during the execution of the half-pass, can only function correctly if the rider has learnt to feel sensitively, is variable enough with his aids and does not lose sight of the diagonal.

Conclusion of the movement

The half-pass ends on a pre-determined point. At this point, the half-pass either ends or a marker has been reached and the direction of movement needs to be changed.

For the change of direction, the horse is positioned and bent in a supple manner into the new direction of movement. To achieve this, the horse is initially brought to a neutral position parallel to the outside edge of the school through active, straight riding. The rider uses the inside leg, while needing to shift his weight to the other side, re-position himself, and move his shoulders forwards into the new direction of movement fluently and without transition, within one horse's length. During half-pass at the canter, the flying change also needs to be fitted into this phase.

In the case of zigzag half-pass, all the measures described in the preparations need to be repeated again, which can cause the rider to break out in a sweat if the horse is lazy!

Evaluation

The half-pass shows how far the fine-tuned co-operation between horse and rider has advanced and how far the rider has developed a feeling for rhythm. In particular, the rider's aids during the changes of direction are a measure of the actual Durchlässigkeit (suppleness) of the horse on show and its even gymnastics exercises on both sides.

Critical moments

Even if the rider has learnt to keep the diagonal in sight, rides by feel, and has automated his aids, the movement is not very easy. This is because the horse needs to be led precisely and constantly on a line, without an optical point of focus such as the outside edge of the school.

Keeping the hindquarters behind the forehand actually doesn't pose any serious difficulties for most riders. Critical situations are more likely to occur during the moment of introduction and the change of direction, during which the half-pass has to be broken off and re-built in the other direction and within a very short time span. The main point here is, strictly speaking, only the speedy re-positioning to the front of the shoulder. The faster the forehand can be turned into the new direction, the more elegant the half-pass and its transitions look. Therefore, great care should be taken during training once the horse has learnt the preparative shoulder-ins.

Achievable degree of skill

The highlight of achievement of this movement is the zigzag half-pass on the centre line of a large square, demanded in competitions from advanced level onwards. Younger riders and horses initially learn only the half or whole half-pass.

Faults and corrections

The correct execution of a half-pass places high demands on the sensitive, well-tuned effect of the rider's hands when it is necessary to change the transition of the motion energy from one to the other direction and change the position of the horse's neck. Here, as always, riders who pull on the reins, and a resisting horse, will very quickly produce faulty positions and distortion in the region of the poll and neck.

Falling-out through the shoulder

One consequence of faulty positions and distortion in the region of the poll and neck can be that horse develops the fault of falling out through the shoulder.

In principle, a horse can fall out through both shoulders. When performing movements in correct position, the outside shoulder is usually the one affected. Every time the outside rein is incapable of fixing the horse's neck at the base, neck and head duck out to the inside, while the horse escapes to the outside over the insufficiently controlled shoulder. There is no bending of the spine or desired direction of the entire forehand into the direction of movement.

As a consequence, the horse fails to step over enough with its front legs into the direction of movement, because the falling-out outside shoulder tends to move in the other direction. Riders lacking attention often only realise in the second third of the diagonal that their horses no longer move in the direction of the pre-determined point. Unfortunately they often employ the outside spur very heavily, instead of pulling less on the inside rein and using the outside leg increasingly right from the start.

The corrective measure is as clear as the cause. The horse needs to step up to the outside rein, owing to the fact that only this rein, in connection with an outside leg that is not placed too far back, is capable of stabilising the shoulder on the same side, and thereby stopping faults from developing. If the length of the outside rein is correct so that the horse could establish contact, the work of the inside rein and the rider's leg on the same side has not yet achieved the aspired goal of the exercise.

More effective half-halts, which the horse accepts on the bit and which allow the rider's inner leg to come into effect, will ensure that in time the horse will loosen its contact with the inside rein more and more and strengthen contact with the outside rein. With growing dominance, this rein will be able to control the outside shoulder more efficiently.

At the same time, the outside leg is placed forwards close to the girth. This ensures that the drifting outside shoulder is restrained and driven in the direction of the horse's head and that the movement of the hind legs are redirected to the horse's mouth until they reach the outside rein and the horse is straight in itself.

Initially, the growing inclination of the horse corrected in this manner to move its forelegs faster and to fall in the other direction may only be limited through the inside rein with due care. Half-halts which are too harsh would soon rob the horse of the courage to attempt this more distinct lateral tendency and force it to fall back into the old faults or to find new ones.

Lack of bending

As described, the forehand and hindquarters move on two tracks if the movement is executed correctly. On these two tracks the four legs cross over on four track lines. In contrast to the shoulder-in, these specifications cannot only be achieved through a pronounced bending of the horse's spine, which is one of the most important training goals of this movement, but also with rigidly stiff horses without any curvature of the ribcage at all.

The expert immediately recognises stiff horses, in particular those which produce a kink in their neck while lacking any kind of bending in the ribcage, as their forelegs need to cross over just as intensively as their hind legs. This, in the case of a horse with a non-yielding, rigid back, is due to the forehand twisting inwards as soon as the hindquarters are positioned towards the inside. As forehand and hindquarters are now both positioned at the exact same angle in relation to the line, all four legs need to cross over to the same degree.

If the rider's inside leg, in co-ordination with the inside rein, is unable to create a hollow in the ribcage section of the horse and if the outside, retaining leg behind the girth cannot stop the horse's outside hind leg from falling out, the hind legs of the horse will no longer step under the horse's centre of gravity. Instead, they will move predominantly sideways as in leg yielding.

As a rule these are horses trained by riders who haven't yet actually understood the purpose of the "tool" of half-pass. For them the movement is purely an end in itself: the only purpose seems to be to ride the diagonal line as crookedly as possible. It is typical of this kind of riding that the horses are ridden out of the corner correctly but don't show any correct degree of bending after a short time. Instead, they move along the diagonal line stiff and askew until the bend eventually points against the direction of the movement in the same way as the horse moves during leg yielding. Such demonstrations lack the essential characteristics of the movement.

Therefore, it is important during daily training to test not only the theoretical knowledge of the rider with regard to the objective of this movement, but also to fall back on corrective exercises which will effect an improvement of the horse's back. All turns – circles, voltes and serpentines through the whole of the school – are suitable exercises to supple a horse's back.

In order to be able to implement the rider's inside and outside leg more effectively in future, and thereby also improve the bend of the ribcage, shoulder in or riding with counter head position, with frequent transitions to the canter from this exercise are very suitable.

Owing to the lack of bending and consequently a shoulder that does not lead adequately, the horse is unable to cross over its forelegs sufficiently in the direction of the movement.

No rider should attempt to ride half-pass with his horse without proper training and preparation regularity, impulsion and lateral bend are lost, the exercise should be broken off immediately and built up again through one or several voltes.

Leading hindquarters

In their effort to position the hindquarters of the horse parallel to the long side, many riders place their outside leg too far back. Therefore, the hindquarters move out, with greater lateral scope of motion than the forehand, and finally take the lead.

One cause of this is that the rider's outside leg affects the hindquarters more directly than the forehand. On the other hand however, the inside front leg is simply more and more in the way of the outside leg. The outside front leg, which is supposed to cross in front and over the inside one, can no longer follow this requirement because the inside shoulder is positioned next to, or even in front of, the outside shoulder. The outside front leg would now have to practically cross over through the inside leg or behind it. In this case the riders also have the feeling of not reaching the pre-determined point in the school.

The corrective measure is relatively easy. The rider places his outside leg forwards on the girth in order to activate the shoulder and front legs of the horse jointly with the outside rein, until the lateral movements of the forehand and hindquarters have adapted to each other again.

In order to correct horses that already perform this fault from habit, it can help to place the rider's inside leg further back than the outside one. This limits the lateral scope of motion of the hindquarters directly at the hind leg, until the outside rein and leg aids have succeeded in turning the horse around the middle and once more position it correctly in relation to the line.

This also prevents the risk of injuries, which occur almost inevitably if the hindquarters are leading. Owing to the limited chance of movement of both front legs, they often knock each other, which can very easily lead to the formation of splints in the area of the front canon bones and injuries to the ligaments.

Remarks

As a rule, half-pass at the canter is combined with a change of direction that not only requires the complete and rapid re-positioning of a horse but also presumes an impeccable flying change, which needs to be integrated into the movement. Mistakes made during training can no longer be hidden, particularly during the zigzag half-pass, and are almost impossible to correct during the execution of the movement. Faults that occur during the practice of the flying change will consequently regularly occur during the half-pass and make this movement unnecessarily complicated.

The hindquarters of the horse are positioned too far to the inside. Therefore the horse is no longer able to follow the greater lateral scope of motion of the hindquarters with the forehand.

During daily training, the half-pass at the canter and the flying change should be worked on thoroughly and separately. Mastering them reliably is a stringent prerequisite for the successful combination of both exercises.

5. Flying changes

The flying change at the canter is executed correctly if the horse, elevated and with a distinct forward tendency and relaxed and straight in itself, jumps simultaneously further forward with the hitherto outside lateral pair of legs during the moment of the free phase of suspension. It then touches the ground and due to the new bend and correct head position becomes the new inside lateral pair of legs. Rhythm, elevation, and direction of movement do not change either before, during or after the changeover.

In show jumping or cross-country, the flying change is predominantly used to change from one canter lead to the other in as short a time as possible. However, the purpose in advanced dressage competitions is not to disturb the elegant, fluent overall impression of a circuit at the canter, in particular when changing the rein, which would occur, for example, with the simple change of canter.

In addition, of course, flying changes serve to test whether the horse is on the aids. The exercise promotes to a high degree the dexterity, feeling of balance, Durchlässigkeit (suppleness), and responsiveness of the horse, and if executed correctly improves the flexion of the hocks, development of impulsion and power of expression.

The canter is the only pace of the horse that provides it with two different options of motion – not taking into account the faulty disunited canter – with the canter on the left and the right leg. The horse is able to change back and forward between the canter on the left and the right leg via the flying change at almost any time and without interrupting the pace at almost every tempo. This ensures that the horse is able to support itself on the ground even in the tightest turns at a high speed. The flying change in no way influences the sequence of footfalls of the pace, which the horse simply continues after the change with the other lateral pair of legs.

The horse is only able to follow the preparative aids of the rider during contact with the ground before and after the phase of suspension, during the moment of the take-off and landing. Therefore, the precise moment in time during which the rider gives the aids is responsible as in no other movement for the success or lack of success of the flying change.

During the short moment of the phase of suspension, when all four legs of the horse are in the air, the dressage horse resembles the show jumper over a fence, and at this time even the experienced rider is unable to implement any corrective measures. Therefore, correct riding prior to the change and the co-operation of the horse are much more important than the changes of lead themselves, which are really only to be seen as the logical result of the preparations.

During the flying change, the horse remains straight in itself and touches the ground with the changing hind leg under its centre of gravity. Photograph: Horses in Media/Streitpferd

Prerequisites

Prerequisites for the rider

Theoretical foundations

- The rider needs to have absorbed the flying change at the canter with its complicated processes of movement and be able to tell apart the phases of contact with the ground and suspension of his horse theoretically and through sensitivity in the seat.

The seat

- The rider who sits with a straight upper body, which rests on both seat bones and the crotch with the inside seat bone carrying the greater amount of weight, no longer has any problems with the motion of the canter. He is capable of adapting his stable, independent seat to the relatively fast changing circumstances of this exercise.
- During none of the phases of the change of lead may the rider carry out extravagant movements or leave the saddle.

Prerequisites for the horse

Physiological foundations

- Depending on its state of training and its ability to collect itself, the horse has a neck with a good to very good elevation which carries itself and is steady at the base. The horse canters well-rounded, completely relaxed, and perfectly straight in itself.

On the aids

- The horse needs to be sensitive enough to perform a correct transition to the canter with the lightest of aids and has to be trained evenly at the canter on both the left and the right leg.
- The counter canter is consolidated. Frequent and correctly ridden simple changes via the walk have adequately stabilised the Durchlässigkeit (suppleness) and balance. The horse has achieved a certain ability to collect itself at the canter.

Execution

Preparatory exercises

The flying change is a completely independent exercise. It is therefore not possible to initially change the lead bit-by-bit – the change is either a change from the start or not a change at all. Unfortunately there is no exercise that leads to it, such as arriving at the shoulder-in automatically through riding with a slight inside bend with continuing training and improvement. Therefore, preparing a young horse for the first flying change under the rider does not differ significantly from the preparations for all further executions of this movement.

The quality of the canter is decisive for the quality of the flying change. Therefore, the improvement of the canter and the quality of the horse's reactions to the aids in general are the most important factors during preparation.

The movement becomes significantly easier to perform if the canter stride is straight, square, energetic, and achieved through barely indicated aids, and can be changed through the paces. Therefore, all exercises and transitions that work towards this goal are also suitable in principle to prepare for the flying changes.

As the horse's shoulder needs to be re-positioned forwards to lead after the flying change, the exercises shoulder-fore and shoulder-in, particularly performed at the canter, have an especially important task during the preparation.

The counter canter on curved lines such as, for example, circles or serpentines, is strenuous for the horse and, in connection with simple changes, explains the wish of the rider to effect the change as a flying change in mid-air. Correctly ridden lateral movements also, as a rule, prepare the horse perfectly for the point of change, so that the resulting flying change can be viewed more as a logical consequence and, of particular importance, becomes a total success from the very first attempt.

Preparation for the movement

The development of the flying change, from the shortened or collected canter, is possible at any point of the school, on each straight or curved line, as a single change or à tempi. However, it is predominantly demanded on the point of change of the diagonal before the canter becomes a counter canter, from the counter canter at the middle of the short sides, or from the normal canter to the counter canter on the middle of the long sides. In addition, the typical points of change are also the centre line, in the case of serpentines through the school, or changes from one circle to another. The flying change is also demanded from the middle canter, usually on the diagonal at the X marker. During show jumping and cross-country, ideally the rider allows the horse to change to the new inside canter before each turn.

The dressage horse that reacts perfectly to the aids - bent and positioned laterally and at the same time straight in itself - will be prepared through half-halts and brought to chew on the bit thoroughly. The elements rhythm, elevation, and self-support need to be established to the extent that they are maintained during the short moment of the change of lead without any significant influence by the rider, and the horse has the opportunity to execute the movement undisturbed.

The aids

The aids for flying changes essentially correspond to those of the transition to the canter. The rider has time until the end of the last stride of the canter before the planned flying change, in other words during the landing phase, to change the position of his leg quickly but not too hastily. For this purpose he simultaneously moves the hitherto inside, forward-driving leg on the girth back a hand's width into the retaining position, while the hitherto outside, retaining leg slips forwards onto the girth. It is not that important when exactly he starts this. More important is that the horse waits and does not jump into the uncompleted aid.

The changing lateral pair of legs jumps forward simultaneously; the distinct forward motion is maintained. The aids of the rider should be less extravagant. Photo Stroscher

With his new inside forward-driving leg on the girth, the rider drives the horse's lateral pair of legs forwards during the moment of the free phase of suspension to change over. Meanwhile, the outside leg, lying a hand's width behind the girth, prevents a falling out and twisting away of the hindquarters.

Both reins also continue to control elevation and chewing on the bit during the phase of the immediate change, but otherwise remain passive in order not to disturb the efforts of the horse in jumping upwards to effect the change.

Conclusion of the movement

The further the new inside hind leg of the horse is extended forwards and jumps under, the more distinct the rider can feel the new bend of the ribcage of the horse. Through re-positioning of the cervical spine, the rider finally adapts the position of the head to the bend. If the rider has a relaxed, independent seat, the weight of the rider and the horse is distributed automatically to the new inner side. This is because the hind leg that is jumping further forward lowers the hip of the horse on the same side, and is felt by the rider via the spine and saddle. After the horse has touched the ground with the new inside hind leg, following the change of lead, and has been re-positioned, collected and stabilised with the outside rein, the rider repeats the aids and half-halts that were necessary for the preparation of the change – either to get the horse to work again calmly or as the best preparation for the next flying change.

Evaluation

The flying change allows the expert the opportunity to evaluate immediately whether the canter on the left and the right legs have been trained equally well and whether horse and rider are able to maintain their rhythm and the line before and after the change in a relaxed manner. It is also interesting to observe to what extent the quality of the change matches that of the canter itself. Even though the change should be executed with elevation and good forward extension, it should not appear as an aberration but is integrated into the canter as a natural component.

Critical moments

As a rule, no critical moments occur if the horse is perfectly on the aids, the training routine has been well phased and the rider has sufficient patience. They are usually only caused through the faults described as follows.

Some riders have difficulty placing the flying change precisely at the required point. In the same way as some show jumping riders complain that they never see a stride, the problem is usually the same for dressage riders, namely the canter itself. Strides that are too long don't allow a better division of the distance to be covered. An unsuitable following of the required line or a horse, which is insufficiently on the aids, can also be partly responsible for this problem. Riders, who can execute the simple change of lead at the required point without a problem, have hardly any difficulty in performing the flying change where it belongs.

Fying changes applied too frequently and without giving any thought to the practicality for the horse, can also work against the rider. This is particularly true if the counter canter has not been consolidated yet. Horses that find the work too strenuous will continue to change back to the inside canter.

The simple solution is to decrease the number of flying changes executed and work intensively on the counter canter. Instead, the usually inexperienced rider desperately tries to prevent the threatened change of lead by means of various contortions. Once the horse has found out how easy it is to evade the counter canter and to confuse the rider, it will have great fun annoying him in future by changing the lead ever earlier.

The only way to correct this is to re-build the horse's training concept with consistency – and that includes the disciplinary aspect. Normal and counter canter should immediately be ridden again with vigour and with more elevation on the outside rein, so that a neck formation steady at the base can guarantee the necessary stability of the shoulder which the majority of such horses tend to drift across. Initially the rider should not ride tight turns at the counter canter, while those performed at the leading canter strengthen the horse's inside hind leg and encourage it to jump further under the horse's body.

If such horses continue to change the lead despite a good preparation and correctly placed legs, vigorous measures will become imperative. Care must be taken, however, that the correction is never directed against the change itself – after all it is still required – but instead against the misbehaviour. A horse which, for example, leans heavily on the reins in order to carry out its tomfoolery will quickly understand through immediate transitions to the walk and rapid resumption of the work at the canter that the time for fooling around is over.

Achievable degree of skill

Apart from improvements to the individual changes, which find their expression in an experienced and more elevated overall picture, the highest degree of skill is the flying change at the canter à tempi. This is in principle a series of individual high quality flying changes that follow each other in series (sets of 1,2,3 or 4 strides on one rein, then the changeover and back over a pre-determined distance).

Faults and corrections

The canter is a three-beat and six phases pace full of impulsion. The horse's inside pair of legs stride further forward than the outside pair. The observer can see the difference between the canter on the left and right rein quite well because of this. The sixth phase is the so-called phase of suspension. The horse can only execute the flying change correctly during this phase. Thus, the moment of the phase of suspension has to coincide perfectly with the change of legs.

Faults occur when the rider makes it impossible for the horse to push itself far enough off the ground in order to have the necessary time for the flying change. Problems also occur if the slow, insufficiently exercised, hind legs require more time for the changeover than the time that the phase of suspension offers.

In the first case, the take-off power needs to be improved, for example, through free jumping, jumping gymnastics and cavalletti work – strong hind legs can push off from the ground distinctly better. In order to encourage the hind legs to jump under the body faster and to increase the flexion of the hocks through exercising, exercises such as the transition into canter from the halt and reining back, as well as smaller turns at the canter, offer a solution. The faster the horse's legs can subsequently perform the change of lead, the shorter the phase of suspension of the collected canter can then become.

Delayed change of the hindquarters or forehand

During the delayed change of the hindquarters or forehand the new forwards striding lateral pair of legs do not change together, during one phase of suspension. Instead the horse requires several phases of suspension during which it usually changes the front leg first and then follows with the hind leg after one or several strides. In rarer cases the hind leg changes first and the front leg follows.

In both cases the rider can clearly feel that his horse is initially moving at the disunited canter and only lands on the intended canter after two or more canter strides. In most cases, these are horses that are held far too low and tightly during the flying change and that are resting on the rider's hands. Rarer, and as a rule more easy to correct, are horses that have gone above the rein and don't dare to jump forwards properly. A slight increase of tempo just before the intended change and a slightly freer basic tempo are usually sufficient to execute the exercise correctly.

For the rider who is not yet very experienced, it is initially not very easy to judge whether his horse has changed legs late at the front or at the back, without a mirror. The expert rider recognises that the horse needs to change behind through the almost normal feeling during the change and the missing conclusion. Alternatively, he is jolted around in the saddle until the very dominant feeling of the flying change occurs one or several strides later.

Any fault during the horse's training can be responsible for the delayed change of the hindquarters or forehand. Often the aids are given too roughly, at the wrong moment and with far too much exertion of the rider's body. In all cases a better preparation of the horse, which ensures that tensions in particular in the back and hind leg are prevented, will correct the fault. A slight increase of tempo from the collection into the changes will also help.

The most frequent cause of the problem is that the movement is practised much too early during the course of training the horse as well as the rider. Accordingly, the prerequisites such as collection, self-support, balance, the moment of applying the aids and the behaviour of the rider during the change need to be checked first and improved if necessary. This method will also often improve the horse's trust in its rider.

The horse that leans on the reins and does not carry itself tends to delay the change of the hindquarters. The hind leg of the changing pair of legs only changes over one or several canter strides after the front leg.

Crooked changes

One of the most frequently demonstrated faults is that of a crooked change. During the moment of the flying change the horse is no longer straight in itself but instead crooked. The haunches turns to the inside and the leading hind leg does not touch the ground under the horse's body, but in a lateral arc next to it.

The causes can be a rider's leg, which is placed too far back and drives the hindquarters inward in the same

The hindquarters of this horse drift to the inside. The hind leg does not touch the ground underneath the horse's body but instead laterally next to the body.

way as a half-pass, or a shoulder, which is insufficiently positioned forwards and practically encourages the hindquarters to swing inwards. It is also possible that too

tight a rein prevents the change from developing sufficiently forwards. In each case, with the crooked change, the horse demonstrates that the time of the phase of suspension is too short for its usually stiff hind legs to be able to jump in a straight line under the centre of gravity.

During this fault, which is easy to feel, the rider has the sensation of a chair being pulled out laterally from under him, with a sharp jerk. Even the inexperienced observer cannot miss this fault – in particular if the horse is changing legs à tempi.

In the most cases, the corrective measures are relatively simple: to start off with the rider needs to ensure that the horse executes the change tension-free. In addition, the horse should be positioned in the other direction before being allowed to jump over. Here, the rider places the forehand in front of the hind leg before the change is executed and this makes a straight changeover distinctly easier to perform. In addition, the new inside rein gets more time to control the poll and then lengthens earlier to create more space for the lateral pair of legs to stride well forwards, and under the body.

The crooked flying change of rein only becomes unpleasant when the fault has become entrenched and has become the norm for the horse. The rider's leg, which should to be placed backwards for the corrective measure, is actually required in front of the girth for a flying change. Very experienced riders give the counter aid at the moment of the change, similar to the introduction of the flying change at every stride. In other words, the inside leg is placed back into the retaining position behind the girth very quickly, even before the horse touches the ground. This is an extremely complicated task because if the corrective aid is given too early, the flying change doesn't happen at all, and if the aid is given too late, the horse has already touched the ground with the lateral pair of legs. Corrective measures can include shoulder-in at the canter, counter canter, flying changes on the circles (in particular from the normal to the counter canter), which all ensure that the horse, in its predicament, does not start to delay changing the legs behind.

Jumping through the shoulder

As in all other movements the horse can also fall out through the shoulders during the flying change at the canter. Usually the new outside shoulder is affected. This fault also leads to crooked changes and again in this case, it is probably impossible for the rider to maintain straight lines.

The cause of this is almost always a completely overbent, usually unstable, neck that finds no support in the insufficiently working outside rein, which is supposed to limit the position of the head, and therefore cannot be securely set at the base. The fault is intensified if the rider places his outside leg too far back.

To solve the problem, the rider needs to stop pulling on the inside rein and instead, give with the inside hand and keep both hands completely neutral during the moment of the change. In stubborn cases, the fault may need to be corrected through riding forwards into the reins with minimum positioning of the head to the outside, at least with good steady contact on the outside rein. In addition, the rider needs to check his application of his outside, retaining leg. If the leg is placed too far back, it not only leaves the rein on the same side to its own devices, but in addition encourages the hindquarters to jump inwards into the centre of the school.

High croup

Jumping up, lifting the hindquarters is primarily a sign of insufficient elevation of head and neck and should not be confused with the horse kicking out against the spurs. Again, this fault means the horse will or cannot stride sufficiently forwards under the body with a hind leg. Instead of flexing the hocks, the horse obtains more time and room to be able to jump forwards more easily, or at all, with its stiff hind leg, by throwing up the hindquarters, often in connection with a short phase at the trot. In other words, the phase of suspension was too short.

Recognition of this also offers the actually quite simple corrective measure: more active rider's legs and more effective half-halts during the preparative work at the canter will lead to better results in a relatively short time. The elevation is improved, the hocks flex, the hind legs become faster and thereby remain close to the centre of gravity more easily, so that the extension forwards is shorter for the changing hind leg. In addition, the rider will be able to feel the individual phases of the stride of the canter more intensely, which will lead to a distinctly better and calmer application of the aids.

Delayed changeover

Faults that impair the seat and aesthetics the most also include the delayed changeover or hesitation before the flying change, even if afterwards, mechanically speaking, the changeover wasn't incorrect and the canter before and after cannot be faulted. The rider gets a feeling that his horse has frozen in the air for a short moment before touching the ground again at the correct canter. Thus, the change does not fit harmoniously into the course of the motion, but is an almost entirely separate movement. For this reason the corrective measure requires a high degree of sensitivity and experience. It is in no way sufficient to increase the rhythm, as is often observed. In this case, the horse simply falls apart, the rider's seat becomes bad, the effect of the aids becomes hazy, and the risk of injuries increases. In addition, experienced horses will still be able to put on the brakes at the last moment and to twist themselves completely, after which they rush for their life again.

On closer examination, the cause of this fault can often be traced back like a red thread through all the other movements. In many cases, the horses are not on the driving aids but evade them – and this is also the relatively

The horse that does flying changes with a too high croup pushes off the ground with insufficiently flexed hindquarters in order to gain space for the changing hind legs, which also lack the desired flexion of the hock and fetlock joints.

simple corrective measure. All exercises and transitions, but in particular the canter, need in future to be ridden under the understanding that the rider has to achieve a much increased sensitivity of the horse towards the leg aids within a short space of time. This improved Durchlässigkeit (suppleness), in particular towards the forward-driving leg, allows the rider to continue to move off at a well-grounded tempo. The rider needs to drive the horse forwards only at the precise moment at which the horse wants to slow down during the phase of suspension. It is imperative, therefore, to maintain the tempo at the canter so that the flying change is performed forwards and upwards from the existing canter.

Running away

Running away, bolting or even just acceleration immediately after the flying change is usually a sign of fear and corresponds to the natural behaviour of the horse as an animal of flight. These horses have often been overtaxed with unsuitable corrective measures regarding possibly faulty changes and they now directly connect the rough application of aids by the rider with the change of lead.

The majority of horses follow the same pattern of behaviour. They tuck their heads in, put their weight on the reins or raise their heads above the reins, hollow their backs and use the change, as it were, as a jumping board in order to push off the ground with stiff hind legs. Once they are on the run, it is very difficult to stop them – with regard to planned tempi changes, basically a catastrophe.

The appropriate corrective measure is predominantly to eliminate the cause of fear in the horse. To do this it is necessary to ensure that Durchlässigkeit (suppleness), an active mouth, control of the poll, and elevation, is secured by actively riding half-halts to such an extent that the aids are understood by the horse in future, even immediately before and after the flying change. Until this has been achieved, the rider should not attempt any more changes. Later, rarely performed and well-executed flying changes, which are praised by the rider, also promote trust and help the horse understand that any attempt to flee is unnecessary.

Refusal to co-operate

This is a fault that can only be eliminated with extreme difficulty when dealing with clever and unco-operative horses. These horses have learned that the rider actually has no options to mechanically enforce a correct flying change of canter. Many a rider has been brought back to earth with a bump by this realisation and it has taught him long forgotten humbleness. Irrespective of whether the horse tenses up and refuses to co-operate from fear or insubordination, the result is the same: the aids for the flying change are simply ignored.

Finding the reason for this behaviour is the only chance to be able to apply the corrective measure. Initially, it will be the correct thing in both cases to categorically dispense with asking the horse to perform flying changes for a certain amount of time until the horse has gained more trust or has developed a higher degree of discipline and Durchlässigkeit (suppleness) through respective corrective work. Practical experience shows that such horses also refuse to co-operate in other aspects where it is easier to correct faults. Therein lies the starting point for any corrective work. Once this problem has been solved, the horse will, in most cases, perform the flying change as a matter of course and without resistance.

Any application of force or attempt to try to enforce the flying change in the corners of the school or over poles on the ground is completely wrong. It is not the flying change of lead in itself that is causing problems for the horse – after all any foal will perform perfectly natural and spontaneous flying changes in the field only a few days after birth. Force will only drag the rider back even further and he is likely to experience the entire scale of possible faults until he has destroyed the last vestige of trust the horse ever demonstrated.

Remarks

As a rule, the show jumping or cross-country rider uses the flying change to change from one canter to the other in order to maintain the necessary balance in a turn, or to conserve the horse's strength if it is showing signs of fatigue. Normally these riders ask for the flying change at a different basic tempo than the dressage rider. However, the same rules apply even with the jumping seat and at a fast tempo – disunited flying changes not only increase the risk of injury but also cost much time and energy.

The rider should not attempt the flying change at the medium canter until the horse can perform the movement faultlessly at the collected canter. It is sufficient to gradually increase the basic tempo over a period of time. This principle also applies fully to the training of show jumpers or cross-country horses ridden with the jumping seat.

6. Tempi changes

Flying changes at the canter à tempi (or tempi changes) is the term for a certain number of flying changes for a pre-determined number of strides on a given line. They are ridden correctly if they are performed at an evenly maintained tempo and the correct number of strides in the rhythm of the canter strides, straight, with elevation, upwards and with a distinct forward motion.

Tempi changes are demanded exclusively in advanced dressage competitions up to Grand Prix. They present a clear picture of the advanced training status of the dressage horse.

The movement promotes to a high degree dexterity, feeling of balance, Durchlässigkeit (suppleness) and responsiveness of the horse and, if executed correctly, improves the flexion of the hocks, the development of impulsion and power as well as power of expression of the flying change at the canter. If the work is carried out professionally and with care, the tempi changes also strengthen the nerves and composure of the horse.

Tempi changes can, in principle, be ridden with any number of strides per series. The younger the horse, the more strides need to be ridden on one rein between the individual changes. In the case of fully trained horses, the number of strides at the canter between the flying change is

Tempi changes need to be performed rhythmically, straight, and upwards with a distinct forward motion.
Photograph: Stroscher

reduced so that in the end the horse changes at each stride. At shows, the tempi changes are demanded every four, three, or two strides at the canter, in other words four, three, or two tempi or as a flying change from stride to stride.

Prerequisites

Prerequisites for the rider

Theoretical foundations
- The rider needs have absorbed the flying change at the canter with its complicated processes of movement. He must be able to withstand any temptation to ask the horse to do too much, too early, owing to his consolidated realisation that only a canter that is fully developed and collected in every way permits a good change of lead.

The seat
- The rider who sits with a straight upper body that rests on both seat bones and the crotch with the inside seat bone carrying the greater amount of weight no longer has any problems with the flying change at the canter. He is capable of adapting his stable, independent seat to the relatively fast changing circumstances of this movement.
- During none of the phases of the change of lead should the rider in the saddle carry out extravagant movements or come unstuck.
- The rider is capable of reacting reflex-like with his seat if the horse suddenly attempts to transfer its weight onto the bit.

Prerequisites for the horse

Physiological foundations
- Depending on the state of training and its ability to collect itself, the horse has a neck with a good to very good elevation that carries itself and is steady at the base. The horse canters well rounded, perfectly straight in itself, and completely relaxed.

On the aids
- The horse needs to be sensitive enough to perform a correct transition to the canter with the lightest of aids and to be able to perform a flying change in either direction without delay.
- The horse has been trained absolutely evenly at the canter on both the left and right leg and has a pronounced willingness to co-operate with its rider.

Execution

Preparatory exercises

The tempi changes consist of combinations of collected canter strides and flying changes, which are combined in series. This means inevitably that the preparative measures for the first tempi changes for a young horse are, in principle, the same as those for individual flying changes. If one further takes into consideration that the quality of the canter is decisive for the quality of the changes, the preparatory exercises can only be concerned with the improvement of the canter and of the general schooling of the horse being on the aids.

The movement becomes significantly easier to perform if the canter stride is straight, square, and energetic, achieved through barely indicated aids for the canter and can be changed through the paces. Therefore, all exercises and transitions that aim in this direction are suitable in principle, to also prepare for the tempi changes.

As the horse's shoulder needs to be re-positioned forwards to lead after the flying change, the exercises shoulder-fore and shoulder-in, particularly performed at the canter, have an especially important task during the preparation.

Tempi changes are nothing more than riding a number of high-quality flying changes at the canter in a row. The condition of the horse also has a big role to play so it is advised to carry out gradually increasing conditioning work. If the rider doesn't have long forest tracks at his disposal to promote regularity and rhythm, he can also ride the changes with an optional number of strides on a circle, with its infinitive lines, and school the sense of balance of his horse at the same time.

Preparation for the movement

The development of the tempi changes starts from the collected canter, usually on the diagonal, on the long sides of the school or on the centre line. For the purpose of training, and in order to improve the balance of the horse, it is highly recommended to perform tempi changes not only on circles but on all other curved lines as well.

The dressage horse that reacts perfectly to the aids is bent and positioned laterally and at the same time straight in itself. It will be prepared through half-halts and brought thoroughly onto the bit. The elements rhythm, elevation and self-support need to be established to an extent that they are maintained during the short moment of the change of lead and during the strides in between without any significant influence of the rider, and the horse has the opportunity to execute the movement undisturbed.

The aids

The aids for flying changes are essentially identical with those of the transition to the canter – the same as for the individual flying change. During the latter stage of the last stride of the canter before the planned flying change, in other words during its landing phase, the rider changes the position of his leg quickly, but not too hastily. For this purpose he simultaneously moves the hitherto inside, forward-driving leg on the girth back a hand's width into the retaining position, while the hitherto outside, retaining leg slips forwards onto the girth. With his new inside forward-driving leg on the girth, the rider drives the horse's lateral pair of legs forwards during the moment of the free phase of suspension to change over. Meanwhile the outside leg, lying a hand's width behind the girth, prevents a falling out and turning away of the hindquarters. Both reins also continue to control elevation and chewing on the bit during this phase but otherwise remain passive.

After the horse has changed the canter, the rider leads the new inside shoulder of the horse in front of the inside hind leg, changes the horse's bend, and positions his upper body correspondingly to ensure that the horse canters steadily and with elevation on the new outside rein. The rider needs to use the few strides at the canter before the next change to bring the horse back on the seat aids and keep it there through suitable half-halts in order to be able to give the following change of lead the necessary expression with light forward-driving aids. Depending on its temperament, he will therefore have to hold the horse back between the changes or drive it forwards energetically. These aids are repeated until the tempi series is completed.

Conclusion of the movement

After the horse has concluded the last tempi change, the rider positions his shoulders and those of the horse in front of the new inside hind leg, changes the bend of the horse, and maintains it straight in itself with the aid of the new outside rein. If necessary, half-halts are used to contain the tempo of the horse and calm it down so the rider is able to use the forward-driving aids again.

Evaluation

To the expert observer, the tempi changes demonstrate to what degree of sensitivity the horse and rider have been trained. While there is adequate time for preparation and conclusion during the individual single flying change, the pre-determined number of strides during tempi changes determine the space of time that is available for the application of the aids and reaction. While the rider has at least two landing phases during the change after two strides to apply corrective measures, the changes from stride to stride only allow a short moment of applying the aids – and that can become very short for some horses.

Critical moments

If the horse is well on the aids and the rider executes the exercise sparingly and with the necessary patience, critical moments should really not occur at all. If they do, they are usually caused by the faults described below. These, however, are so disturbing that the rider cannot bring his achieved feeling for the movement in harmony with the rhythm of the movement, in particular during the tempi changes from stride to stride. The changes however are not only a question of the rider's feeling, but also a question of the Durchlässigkeit (suppleness) of the horse. After all, the rider's sensitivity needs to be transmitted to and felt by the horse via the aids.

Energetic horses, with a high potential for elevated and extended movement and a talent for understanding the rider, begin to get bored very quickly and become inattentive. In particular, horses that are fully trained to perform tempi changes from stride to stride like to perform these changes with a number of strides which the rider did not actually want to execute in the first place. Some horses start moving down the diagonal of the school with a tempi change from stride to stride and continue this to its conclusion without taking the slightest notice of the protesting rider.

In this case, the horse should only be corrected if it feels uneven and resisting, because it is putting its weight on the reins, for example. The horse needs to get the feeling that the slightly more pronounced aids do not relate to the changes in themselves, in order not to endanger the good co-operation between horse and rider. A suitable corrective measure, for example, is to begin riding the flying change in series of four strides and continue these during the second half of the line as tempi changes for three or two strides. This will disconcert the horse slightly and it will start to concentrate on the rider's aids again very quickly.

Achievable degree of skill

Apart from improvements which relate to a more experienced and more elevated overall expression, the peak of the achievable degree of skill is tempi changes from stride to stride, on straight and curved lines.

Faults and corrections

Typical faults occur if the space of time of the phase of suspension is insufficiently long for the lateral pairs of legs to change fluently. In particular, in the case of tempi changes, the rider then needs to bring the horse back into the optimum state within only a few strides after each flying change, or maintain this in the case of tempi changes from stride to stride, to ensure a powerful propulsion from a very good flexion of the hocks of the leg that pushes off the ground.

In principle, the same faults are possible when performing the tempi changes that can also occur in the case of single flying changes or during normal work at the canter.

Delayed change of the hindquarters or forehand

During the delayed change of the hindquarters or forehand, the new forwards striding lateral pair of legs do not change together during one phase of suspension. Instead the horse requires several phases of suspension during which it usually changes the front leg first and then follows with the hind leg after one or several strides. In rarer cases the hind leg changes first and the front leg follows.

If the fault occurs only in one direction, for example always during the change from the left to the right, the cause is either that the initial canter was not well executed or that the rider disturbed his horse during the moment of the flying change. While the corrective measure is obvious in the first case, an experienced trainer will have to intercept in the second case. If the rider already demonstrates his fault during normal canter work, the trainer will be able to give corrective help over a longer space of time. If the fault, in the rider's seat or application of the aids, only occurs during the moment of the change, the only thing the rider can really do is to practise on an older, experienced horse which won't be confused by the rider. In this way he does not teach his own horse further faults originating from his own initial inability.

The delayed change of the hindquarters or forehand becomes a very real problem when only a few, or in the end no, strides at the canter are provided for between the individual changes – inevitably the horse will then become mixed-up. If the flying changes are otherwise good and the canter is suitable for this exercise, the only recommendation really is patience and to begin with a greater number of strides at the canter between the changes.

Crooked changes

One fault that occurs particularly frequently in the case of tempi changes is the crooked change. During the moment of the flying change the horse is no longer straight in itself but crooked. The haunches swing to the inside as they are meant to during the travers, the leading hind leg does not touch the ground in a straight line under the body of the horse but touches down laterally next to it.

If the horse does not demonstrate this fault in the case of a single flying change at the canter, we must assume that in the eagerness of training, a number of basic rules went out of the window.

In addition to an insufficiently forwards leading shoulder, the cause can also be a rider's leg which is placed far too far back and which causes the hindquarters to swing in towards the centre of the school, much like during the travers. Before the horse becomes even more crooked during the course of the tempi series, the observer will often notice the fidgety seat of the rider. Unable to give the aids in time, because in the case of a low number of strides his legs need to move alternatively too far backwards and forwards at every change, he will therefore stiffen up. Usually it is sufficient to let the rider know so he becomes conscious of this fault and quickly corrects it. If, on the other hand, such distinct leg aids are necessary to induce the horse to carry out the flying change in the first place, the rider should temporarily abstain from performing tempi changes to ensure that the horse reacts more sensitively to the aids of the rider's legs.

Another reason for this fault can be an insufficiently giving rein, which prevents the horse from moving forwards far enough and prevents a straight forwards jumping movement of the lateral pair of legs. Horses that get excited during the course of the tempi changes and have the tendency to start hurrying, tend to strengthen this inflexible rein. Half-halts, which are not relaxed and supple enough, or not applied at all, tend to induce the rider to pull on the bit. Depending on how supple the horse is in the poll and neck area, this can lead to a completely faulty posture of the neck formation. It is clear that there is no sense in this case to continue to work directly on the tempi changes. It is far more sensible to initially check and improve the Durchlässigkeit (suppleness) of the half-halts. Particularly suitable for this task are appropriate transitions, for example from the canter to the halt.

Irrespective of the cause underlying the crooked change, the horse demonstrates with this fault that the time of the phase of suspension is too short for the usually stiff hind legs to jump in a straight line under the centre of gravity of the horse. The feeling in the saddle reminds one occasionally of a swaying boat.

Refusal to co-operate

There are quite a number of horses that will perform the individual flying change obediently but will refuse to co-operate when it comes to the tempi changes – in particular when the number of strides between the changes is reduced. In most cases the reason for this is that the rider progresses too quickly during the training of the horse. Whereas many riders are able to sit relatively stable in the saddle and give the correct aids in the case of four and three strides per change à tempi, they start having problems in the case of two strides and at the flying change from stride to stride. Riders usually recognise that the horse is getting out of control at this stage. However, instead of breaking off the exercise at this point and going back to thinking through and improving the preparative work again, they only aggravate the indistinct application of the aids through increased use of the body.

Their horses become confused by this and in their desperation produce all kinds of possible faults, which lead to further punishment. Only very few horses have the ability to practically sense what the rider wants. Most others damage their nervous system, which has been subjected to this unsatisfactory training method over days or weeks. Depending on their character, some horses seek refuge in flight or in other bad habits from rearing to putting their tongue over the bit as soon as they sense an aid for a flying change. Others simply stop doing anything at all and refuse to co-operate completely.

Only a strong rider may be able to induce such a horse to co-operate again with the help of precise aids. As soon as the aids become lighter in the case of experienced riders no later than when performing tempi changes from stride to stride, the old problem can reoccur. In this case the only correct way forward is a complete re-schooling of the horse over a period of weeks with regard to discipline, trust, and being on the aids. Riding the occasional single flying change at the canter will tell the rider to what extent the horse is prepared to co-operate once more. It should go without saying that the following tempi changes may only be ridden very shortly, very rarely, and with the utmost restraint as a kind of "test".

Remarks

It is a memorable occasion for every rider when he first successfully performs tempi changes with his horse, possibly even flying changes from stride to stride. The extent of elevation and rhythm of this exercise are to be found nowhere else. However, the tempi changes will only be performed full of expression, beautifully and with upward motion if the horse can be seen to enjoy the exercise. Here, as ever, an economical application and much praise are the basis for a harmonious effect.

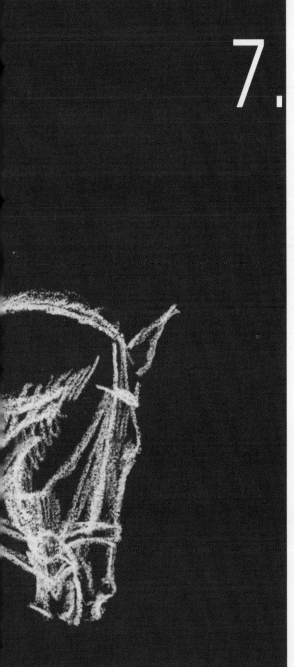

7. Walk pirouette

This movement is executed correctly if a horse with a good elevation, correct head carriage, and bent and positioned laterally in the direction of movement, moves around the lowered hindquarters with the forehand in the distinct four-beat of the collected walk. The front legs move without hurrying, with greater lateral scope of motion on a larger half-circle than the hind legs, which are active on a smaller half-circle. The front legs push the forehand of the horse in an even flow of movement around a point that is as close to the inside hind leg as possible. The inside hind leg steps energetically and rhythmically well under the centre of gravity. The outside hind leg moves beside the inside hind leg, on the same half-circle with the same impulsion and rhythm with the minimum of space, and without crossing over.

The walk pirouette is aimed at introducing the horse to a predominantly diagonal and collectively acting application of the aids and to promote the contact with the outside rein. In addition, it teaches riders, who have reached a higher level of schooling, more complicated transitions and teaches them the advanced effect of the diagonal aids. The walk pirouette is particularly suitable to impart the feeling of an absolutely controlled forehand and elevation.

In the case of a successful execution, the walk pirouette has a high degree of effect regarding straightness and collection. It completes the horse's obedience, dexterity, and ability to collect itself, trains the load-bearing capacity of the hindquarters and is extremely suitable as a schooling aid for concentration and balance.

During the walk pirouette, the forehand moves around the hindquarters with greater lateral scope of motion and without hurrying. Photograph: Bronkhorst

The walk pirouette can be demanded and ridden as a half pirouette (180 degrees) or as full turn (360 degrees). Although the front and hind legs move on two half-circles with different radii, the progress of motion of the four legs is determined by the four beats and eight phases of the walk. With an increasing degree of difficulty of the dressage movements, the walk pirouette is almost routinely demanded as a half pirouette on precisely defined points around or along the outside track of the school until they are almost completely phased out in advanced competitions by canter pirouettes.

Prerequisites

Prerequisites for the rider

Theoretical foundations
- The rider needs to have full theoretical mastery of the not very complicated but almost transiently flowing processes of movement, and needs to be able to apply the inherently logical aids to the horse without hurry and with absolute sensitivity.

The seat
- The rider, who sits initially with a straight upper body that rests equally on both seat bones and the crotch and swings in harmony with the horse at the walk, needs to be able to adapt his independent seat to the relatively slow changing circumstances of this exercise.

This horse is positioned and bent in the direction of movement. The inside hind leg steps underneath the centre of gravity. Photograph: Bronkhorst

- After the introductory half-halt for the actual turn, the rider needs to be able to shift his weight onto the inside seat bone and to align his shoulder axis parallel with that of the horse, without collapsing in the hip.

Prerequisites for the horse

Physiological foundations

- The neck with a good to very good elevation carries itself, is steady at the base and in connection with a free shoulder allows the front legs to cross over almost playfully.

- Muscles and flexion of the hocks of the hindquarters need to be trained to such an extent that they guarantee a dynamic stepping under the centre of gravity, in particular with the respective inside hind leg, on the smallest space possible.

On the aids

- The horse perceives sensitive aids and obeys them without delay.
- The collected walk is fully established.
- The horse is constantly in front of the forward-driving rider's legs, is balanced to a high degree, and is capable of transforming the motion forwards into a lateral motion without a moment's delay.

Execution

Preparatory exercises

The walk pirouette is demanded predominantly in advanced competitions where most riders and horses, due to their experience, have a sufficient number of preparative movements at their disposal. In principle, however, the rider can ensure the necessary attention simply through transitions of tempo within a pace, and teach the horse the aids required for the walk pirouette through exercises with similar diagonal aids. Those that would be suitable include shoulder-fore, circles, or leg-yielding towards the centre of the school and back out after the halfway point, smaller voltes, and turn-about

voltes out of the corner. Exercises that prepare the horse directly are half-turns around the haunches and the turn on the haunches, which are demanded in competitions of a less advanced level, require a less pronounced degree of collection, and are, in principle, the same as a half pirouette.

Preparation for the movement

The walk pirouette is developed from the shortened to the collected walk, depending on the training stage of the horse. The horse, which is straight in itself with a good elevated carriage, is positioned and bent by shortening the inner rein and lifting the rider's inside hand. It is encouraged to come down to chew on the bit. The last metres to the turning point are used to ride the horse discreetly with a tendency towards an increasingly leading shoulder.

Prepared in this way the horse's head carriage is increasingly elevated through the application of half-halts on the outside rein so that all preparations are finished when the shoulder of the horse reaches the turning point. All following aids concentrate solely on the actual turn. The horse is rounded in itself and active with its hind leg and keeps a steady contact as well as elevation.

The rider's legs maintain the walk and the rider moves his shoulder forwards, parallel with the leading position of the horse's shoulder, and thereby turns his upper body to the inside. If the elbows are carried correctly, close to the rider's side, and the lower arms are held independently both will also move to the inside. This means that the inside rein moves to the leading position and in the case of younger horses, even to a sideways indicating position. The outside rein has a strong retaining effect, which limits the correct head position, and under certain circumstances lies against the horse's neck. At the same time the rider's outside leg, lying on the girth, pushes the forehand away from the track into the centre of the school, and thus completes the impulse for the turn.

The aids

The actual turn begins with the reaction of the horse to the preparatory aids, and from now on aids that work on the two diagonals become necessary. Naturally, in practical application, they do not have such a distinctly separate effect as described here for the sake of clarity. They are instead repeated together and intertwined until the half or whole pirouette is completed.

On the first diagonal, the rider's inside leg maintains the gait, in other words it pushes the motion of the walk towards the outside rein which transforms it, closes it, and pushes it to the inside and thereby also helps the inside rein with the turn. On the second diagonal, the rider's outside leg, which is driving the horse forwards and sideways, initially only pushes the horse's forehand. Later, applied behind the girth it also pushes the middle and hindquarters towards the inside rein, which determines the correct head position and leads the horse sideways. In connection with the outside rein it thereby also prevents a turn that is too large. This continues to ensure that the hindquarters are prevented from falling out.

The inside leg on the girth has only one – although the most important – function: it needs to ensure that the momentum is maintained. It is only applied as a corrective measure if the horse starts to hurry and needs to be retained.

While the forehand now begins to move around the hindquarters, and the horse increasingly bends its ribcage, the rider carefully shifts his weight to the inside into the turn, in order to place weight on the inside hind leg, to flex the hock and stay anchored on the spot, so-to-speak. At the same time the hands are busy maintaining the correct head position, elevation and chewing on the bit by means of suitable half-halts on the reins.

Conclusion of the movement

The rider finishes the pirouette by transforming the sideways-forwards movement into a purely forward-driving movement in order to be able to leave the turning point on a straight line. For this purpose, he lightens the weight aid and allows the horse a more expanded frame by lengthening the reins. At the same time he drives it out of the turning with the inside leg and returns to the collected walk. At the end, the rider once more lengthens the inside rein by the amount it was shortened and the laterally driving leg is placed in the normal, forward-driving position on the girth.

Evaluation

To the expert observer the walk pirouette demonstrates to what degree of sensitivity the fine-tuning between horse and rider has developed and what kind of sensitivity of movement the rider has. The rider, in particular at the start of the turn, shows what degree of Durchlässigkeit (suppleness) the horse really has achieved and the work of the hind legs allows conclusions to be drawn as to what extent the horse really was in front of the aids.

Critical moments

The majority of critical moments occur when a forward motion needs to be transformed into a lateral motion, while there should be no difficulties the other way around. In this case, in order to create the correct prerequisites for the horse, it is not only the optimum starting position that is important but also the choice of the correct tempo. On the one hand, this minimises the forces, but on the other care must be taken not to eliminate too much of the horse's own dynamics and expression.

Experience shows that in the case of young horses the preparations need to be executed a bit earlier and in a more pronounced way, and that the horse executes one or two shortened steps before the turn in order to find its balance safely.

Achievable degree of skill

The walk pirouette is the smallest turn that the horse is capable of. An increase in the degree of skill therefore is shown in an improved execution. Furthermore, in relation to the controlled forehand, pirouettes at the walk can also be performed very well as a preparation for lateral movements and, further down the line, for the canter pirouettes.

Faults and corrections

Lack of preparation

In the case of this exercise, precise, timely preparation during the phase of the initial walk is of deciding significance. Any rider, experienced or inexperienced, who does not take this into account and underestimates the walk pirouette will make a severe error, which will manifest itself in hair-raisingly awful turns.

The cause for this may not only be the inconsistency of the horse being on the aids at all times, but also a rider who is insufficiently schooled and often remains sitting inactively on his horse right up to the last moment. These riders have not learned to talk to their horse in the right manner, to induce transitions correctly and to check at which stage of preparation the horse currently is before executing the movement. To eliminate this fault, the rider and horse have to be trained more carefully and more strictly in order to achieve a reliable Durchlässigkeit (suppleness). They should also specifically practise the walk pirouette precisely at a given point and without contact with the outside rail of the school.

Pirouettes that are too large

The pirouette will always become too large if the forehand does not turn around the hindquarters fast enough. This happens in particular if the rider is not able to transform the forward motion sufficiently into a predominantly lateral motion, for example in the case of a horse that kinks its neck at the base, which allows it to fall out over the outside shoulder. All further efforts are thwarted through the uncontrolled forward drive of the horse so that the lateral movement has no chance to come into effect. Pushing hind legs and insufficient collection, paired with a loose, over-bent neck which does not let the rider's half-halts through, make it particularly difficult for the rider to stabilise the forehand and to move it straight into the turn, away from the line. Thus, the forehand does not move around quickly and laterally enough, and the pirouette becomes too big.

All corrective measures that can help improve the Durchlässigkeit (suppleness) on the effect of the outside rein and leg – for example, transitions from canter to walk, rein-back, half-turns around the haunches, crossing over, voltes from the shoulder-in – will provide for a better preparation in the future.

Turn around the middle

A further frequently seen faulty execution of the walk pirouette is the turn around the middle. Forehand and hindquarters swing out laterally in equal parts, the horse turns at its middle. Not placing the inside hind legs forwards, under the centre of gravity, also often produces forwards leaning riders, who attempt desperately to control the horse's weight in the reins, which threatens increasingly to pull them out of the saddle. Some riders are content as long as the horse that leans on the bit with a stiff neck does not propel itself backwards, thereby completely exposing the rider.

The cause of this fault is usually that the rider has braced his back insufficiently or used his outside leg ineffectively, in connection with a strong pull on the inside rein. Any improvement will only show itself when the rider has learned to bend his horse, attained the correct head position, collected it and kept it in front of his driving aids. Exercises such as the crossing over of the horse's legs, shoulder-in, correctly executed reining back, and frequent transitions to the walk or the trot from the halt can support and help.

Cross-over

The horse is likely to cross over with its hind legs if, due to a lack of forward-driving impulses, it does not move its stiff hind legs after the first aid to turn has been given. In the course of the turn, the legs cross over and are seen to dig deeper and deeper into the sand. This unstable support gives the rider the feeling of sitting on a swaying

This horse's hind legs remain standing instead of stepping in the distinct four-beat of the walk. The forward motion in the movement is lost completely.

plank which stretches further and further until it sinks down in the centre and threatens to break apart. The turn is usually concluded in a swaying manner.

Here, as before, all corrective measures that help the hind legs move are suitable. It is correct to apply increasingly forward-driving measures during turns, which are executed distinctly large, if necessary as large as a volte, as long as they only improve the forward extension, contact, and roundness of the horse. It is important to break off the movement by riding straight forwards immediately and to consequently build it up again if the hind legs have come to a halt. For some horses it is helpful and easier to spiral in on a circle, which after the volte, ultimately leads to the pirouette. The aids for the spiral are almost identical and can also be increased until the horse reaches the actual turn. On the way to the centre the rider applying the corrective aids has sufficient time to prepare the horse and wait for the most favourable moment for the pirouette.

Stepping over

Judges and trainers seem to take less and less notice of hind legs that step over one another incorrectly. As in the case of the turn around the middle and of the half-turns around the haunches, the hind legs stepping over one another is not desired throughout the entire course

If the hindquarters are pointed into the centre of the school, as during the travers, the horse will begin to step over the inside hind leg with the outside hind leg.

of the movement. It is only allowed during the final stride in order to help the hindquarters return to the track, if at all. Hind legs that step over not only decrease the ability of the horse to collect itself but also put the work at the walk in question. This action also enlarges the walk pirouette unnecessarily.

Faults occur if the rider pushes the hindquarters into the centre of the school (as in the travers) and the outside hind leg then begins to step over. This stops the work of the laterally working forehand, which cannot move around the hindquarters. Now the demonstration looks more like a lateral race between the forehand and the hindquarters, during which the forehand only seems to get the upper hand with difficulty.

The corrective measure is simple. The rider does not place his outside leg as far back and uses it less actively and it may only have an effect if the horse's inside shoulder is leading distinctly. If the fault has already become entrenched, the rider needs to correct it with his inside leg placed back slightly.

A loose neck as well as hind legs that step over very rarely allows the correct execution of pirouettes ridden on a point. They also tempt the rider to improvise under the pressure of time. In most cases such turns end as unpunctually as they started, and it becomes extraordinarily difficult for the rider to conclude the movement on a straight line.

Horses that are supple and pliable and only difficult to control during the pirouette can execute the pirouette during schooling lessons from the third track in the direction of the corners. This offers the horses a natural boundary in the form of the outside track of the school. After careful preparation, the rider only has to concentrate on keeping the horse in front of his forward-driving legs.

Lack of regularity

With regard to lack of regularity, walk pirouettes can be judged extraordinarily well because the horse usually moves at the collected walk beforehand and the observer gets a feel for the rhythm. Lack of regularity can occur in the case of the slightest disharmony between rider and horse and often even the expert only feels it after the event. As a rule, countermeasures are therefore applied too late and can at best prevent even worse faults. Therefore, only preventative measures that focus on an even more improved Durchlässigkeit (suppleness) of the horse, in connection with a good fine-tuning, can cure this fault permanently. This allows the rider to execute the movement with extremely careful aids so that the horse maintains its outline and the determined tempo almost by itself.

Remarks

A main factor in the successful execution of the walk pirouette is the correct degree of application of the aids, which needs to be matched to the temperament and the mood of the horse on the day. The state of the ground also has a significant influence: deep, heavy going, in particular, makes the work difficult for the horse.

Experienced riders will prefer to aim for larger pirouettes from a freer walk in order to prevent a lack of regularity.

As with all other tight turns, the walk pirouette also places stress on the tendons, joints, and discs of the horse. Therefore, they should only be executed after careful loosening work and not too frequently overall. For good riders, they serve in particular as a check for the correctness of the preparatory work.

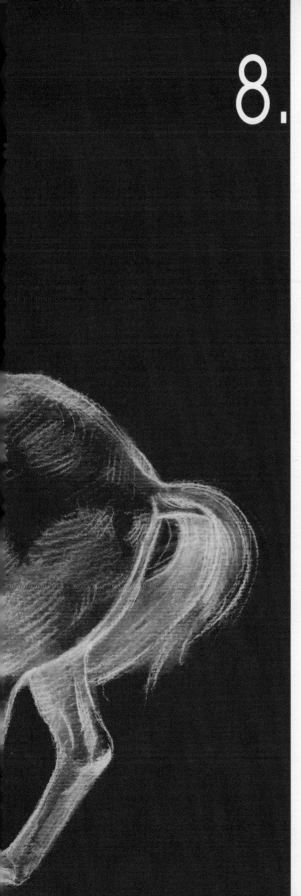

8. Canter pirouette

This movement is executed correctly if a horse with a good elevation, correct head carriage, and bent and positioned laterally in the direction of movement, jumps around its lowered hindquarters, with the forehand in the distinct three-beat of the collected canter. The front legs move with greater lateral scope of motion on a larger half-circle than the hind legs, which are active on a smaller half-circle. Thereby, the forehand of the horse is pushed around a point in an even flow of movement that is as close to the inside hind leg as possible.

The canter pirouette introduces riders who have reached an advanced level of schooling to more complicated transitions and turns. It also teaches them the progressive effect of the diagonal aids, as well as the feeling of an absolutely controlled forehand with high elevation. When successfully executed, the canter pirouette is highly effective in promoting straightness and collection. It completes the horse's obedience, dexterity, and ability to collect itself extraordinarily, trains the load-bearing capacity of the hindquarters, and is extremely suitable as a schooling aid for concentration and balance.

In its perfect execution, the canter pirouette demands the highest level of collection that the horse is capable of. It can be ridden as a half pirouette (180 degrees) or as a full pirouette (360 degrees). Although the front and hind legs move on two half-circles with different radii, the progress of motion of the four legs is determined by the three beats and six phases of the canter. As the dressage movements become more difficult, the canter pirouette is performed exclusively as a full pirouette on precisely defined points and, together with the walk pirouette, represents the smallest possible turn for a horse.

During the canter pirouette, the horse makes a highly elevated jump with its forehand around the lowered hindquarters, which bear the weight. The distinct three-beat of the canter needs to be maintained.
Photograph: Horses in Media/Frieler

Prerequisites

Prerequisites for the rider

Theoretical foundations

- The rider needs to have full theoretical mastery of the not very complicated but almost transiently flowing processes of movement and needs to be able to apply the inherently logical aids to the horse without rushing and with absolute sensitivity.

The seat

- The very stable rider who sits with a straight upper body needs to be able to adapt his independent seat to the relatively fast changing circumstances of this exercise.
- After the introductory half-halt, the rider needs to be able to shift his weight onto the inside seat bone and align his shoulder axis parallel with that of the horse without collapsing in the hip
- If it suddenly tries to support itself by leaning on the bit, the rider is able to correct the horse through reflex-like counter shifting of the weight.

Prerequisites for the horse

Physiological foundations

- The neck, with a good to very good elevation, depending on the degree of training of the horse, carries itself, is steady at the base, and in conjunction with a free shoulder allows the front legs to cross over almost playfully.

- Muscles of the hindquarters and flexion of the hocks need to be trained to such an extent that they guarantee a dynamic jumping under the centre of gravity on the smallest space.

On the aids

- The horse perceives sensitive aids and obeys them without delay.
- The collected canter is fully established; small turns present no problems whatsoever.
- The horse co-operates willingly, is more or less completely in balance, and is therefore capable of transforming the forward motion into a lateral motion without a moment's delay.

Execution

Preparatory exercises

By performing transitions of tempo within a pace, the rider is able to ensure the required attention of the horse and introduce it to the necessary aids for the pirouette by means of movements with similar diagonal aids. These could include shoulder-in, lateral movements, smaller voltes at the canter and turn-about voltes.

Preparation for the movement

Depending on the state of training, the canter pirouette is developed from the well- to very well-collected canter. In competitions, the movement is demanded at precisely defined points on one of the lines of change of rein, on the centre line, or on diagonal lines of the dressage arena.

The horse that is straight in itself, with a good elevation, is positioned and bent by shortening the inner rein and lifting the rider's inside hand. It is encouraged to come down to chew well on the bit. The last metres to the turning point are used to bring the inside shoulder in front of the inside hind leg. This is done in such a manner that the horse remains completely straight within itself, relaxes the contact on the inside rein, and with strong elevation on the outside rein, begins to take up more weight with the hindquarters. The flexion of the hocks achieved in this way guarantees an evenly maintained tension and elevation.

The rider's legs maintain the canter and the rider moves his outside shoulder forwards, parallel with the leading position of the horse's shoulder, and thereby turns his upper body to the inside. If the elbows are carried correctly, close to the rider's side, and the lower arms are held independently, both will also move to the inside. This means that the inside rein moves to the leading position and, in the case of younger horses, even in a sideways indicating position. The outside rein, which lies against the horse's neck, has a strong retaining effect, which limits the correct head position under certain circumstances. At the same time, the rider's outside leg, lying on the girth, pushes the forehand away from the track into the centre of the school, and thus completes the impulse for the turn.

The aids

The actual turn begins with the reaction of the horse to the preparatory aids, and from now on aids that work on the two diagonals become necessary. Naturally, in practical application, they do not have such a distinctly separate effect as described here for the sake of clarity. They are instead repeated together and combined, until the half or whole pirouette is completed.

On the first diagonal, the rider's inside leg maintains the gait, in other words it pushes the motion of the canter towards the outside rein, which takes it up, transforms it into an elevation and pushes it away to the inside, and thereby helps the inside rein with the turn. On the second diagonal, the rider's outside leg behind the girth, which is driving the horse forwards and sideways, pushes the forehand and middle towards the inside rein, which determines the correct head position and leads the horse sideways. In connection with the outside rein it thereby also prevents a turn that is too large. This continues to ensure that the hindquarters are prevented from falling out.

The inside leg on the girth has only one function – albeit the most important: it needs to ensure that the momentum is maintained. It is only applied as a corrective measure if the horse starts to hurry and needs to be retained.

While the forehand now begins to move around the hindquarters and the horse increasingly bends its ribcage, the rider carefully shifts his weight to the inside, into the turn, in order to place weight on the inside hind leg, to flex the hock and stay anchored on the spot, so-to-speak. At the same time, the hands are busy maintaining the correct head position, elevation, and chewing on the bit by means of suitable half-halts on the reins.

Conclusion of the movement

The rider finishes the pirouette by transforming the side-ways-forwards movement into a purely forward-driving movement in order to be able to leave the turning point on a straight line. To achieve this, he lightens the weight aid and allows the horse a more expanded frame by lengthening the reins. At the same time, with the inside leg, he drives the horse out of the turning movement and returns to the collected canter. At the end, the rider lengthens the inside rein once more by the amount it was shortened and the laterally driving leg is placed in the normal, forward-driving position on the girth.

Evaluation

To the expert observer the canter pirouette demonstrates to what degree of sensitivity the fine-tuning between horse and rider has developed and what kind of sensitivity of movement the rider has. The rider's aids, at the start of the turn in particular, show the degree of Durch-lässigkeit (suppleness) the horse really has achieved.

Critical moments

The majority of critical moments occur when a forward motion needs to be transformed into a lateral motion. In this case, in order to create the correct prerequisites for the horse, it is not only the optimum starting position that is important but also the choice of the correct tempo. This, on the one hand minimises the centrifugal forces, but on

the other hand must take care not to eliminate too much of the horse's own dynamics and expression.

Experience shows that in the case of younger hors-es the half-halts required for complete collection and elevation preparations need to be executed a bil more pronounced and earlier, and that the horse executes one or two shortened canter strides before the turn in order to safely find its balance.

Achievable degree of skill

The canter pirouette is the smallest turn that the horse is capable of at the canter. An increase in the degree of skill therefore is shown in an optimised execution with regard to correct head position, bending, elevation, and flexion of the hocks. As they need to be performed several times as tempi changes in daily schooling, the multiple pirouette shown in particular in freestyle competitions, does not in actual fact represent a higher degree of skill.

Faults and corrections

Too large pirouette

The faults described in the case of the walk pirouette, such as the lack of preparation and lack of regularity, will also occur in the case of canter pirouettes.

The canter pirouette becomes too large if the forehand does not turn around the hindquarters fast enough. This happens, in particular, if the horse's head was positioned too early and too far sideways and the neck,

This insufficiently elevated, and at the same time over-bent, horse finds no boundary on the outside rein, which is supposed to lead the forehand into the turn. The rider's lower outside leg, which is placed too far back, allows the hindquarters to jump next to the forehand: the pirouette becomes too large.

which had thereby become much too soft and wavering, was unable to find a reliable boundary in the outside rein. The pirouette will also become too large in cases where the canter is not collected enough, or if a rider's outside leg is placed too far behind the girth, which allows the hindquarters to consistently jump next to the forehand.

All corrective measures that can help improve the Durchlässigkeit (suppleness) on the effect of the outside rein and leg provides for a better preparation in the future. For example, transitions from canter to halt and medium canter to walk, pirouettes at the walk, voltes from the shoulder-in and from lateral movements would all be suitable – and movements which improve the collection, such as the counter canter, the renvers, lateral movements on the circles, and similar exercises. More energetic cantering during the shoulder-in with medium positioning of the head will also ensure that the forehand of the horse can be encouraged permanently to lead more easily – the real purpose of the pirouette.

Too small pirouette

Initially it seems a paradox to state that a pirouette is too small – however, this fault can be observed very frequently. Whereas in the case of a successful pirouette a distinct motion forwards can be seen in each of the four to six strides at the canter, any forwards impulsion seems to have disappeared in the case of the too small pirouette, in fact one can hardly speak of canter strides. The observer gets the impression that the horse seems to burrow itself into the ground with the inside hind leg and only

executes a simple turning movement interrupted by short bounces on the ground with the forehand.

One of the reasons that this fault occurs is if a horse that is stable, even stiff in itself, is pushed into too much elevation and jumps under its body with an incorrectly concave back. In this case, the hindquarters have to take on too much weight and are therefore unable to perform a canter stride. This distinct disproportion between carrying and pushing force not only overtaxes the muscles of the haunches, but also gives the rider the feeling of not being able to come out of the pirouette, because the horse is completely behind the forward-driving aids.

In most cases these horses have been trained by riders who did not have the required patience to build up the pirouette movement. Due to their experience of rough hands and sharp bits, these horses refuse to let the rider drive them onto the bit and cautiously remain behind it. They offer an unreliable contact on the rein which can in some cases be combined with a tongue over the bit.

There is little sense in introducing the pirouette at a higher speed as a corrective measure: often the cause of the fault can be followed through all other movements and shows up in particular during flying changes and the piaffe. The experienced rider will employ a relatively simple corrective measure, which applies to all movements. All movements and transitions, in particular during the canter, are in future ridden in such a way that the horse becomes very much more sensitive to the aids of the rider's legs within a short space of time. This improved Durchlässigkeit (suppleness) allows the rider to continue to perform the pirouette at a steady tempo. Only when the fault actually occurs during the moment of the introduction to

This horse, with an exaggerated elevation, pushes its back down, away from the aids. The hindquarters have to take up too much weight, which makes it almost impossible for them to perform the canter stride. There is no longer any recognisable forward motion.

the turn, when the horse wants to delay, does the rider need to come through with his driving aids. He thus needs to implicitly maintain the tension at the canter before, during, and after the turn, and drive the pirouette forwards in front of his legs so that the horse jumps distinctly better forward-upwards.

The second reason for too small a pirouette is a horse that throws itself out through the inside shoulder in the turn. These horses often try to pull against the hands with a neck held too low, and to dive under the reins. It is difficult for the rider to stabilise the forehand and to

maintain the positioning of the neck to the inside and at the same time counteract the pressure on the rein with his seat. As the forehand swings around much too fast and the horse canters downhill with stiff hind legs, high hindquarters, and supporting its weight on the forehand, the rider feels exposed to an immense turning movement and the danger is that he will fall forwards, which would only exacerbate the fault.

Apart from problems with balance and conformation faults, the cause of this fault can also lie in an insufficiently developed load-bearing capacity of the hind legs, lack of collection and elevation, or simply a pulling rider's hand. It is possible not only to feel and see the fault but in most cases also to hear it, because the hoofs of the overloaded forelegs clash against each other and the horse frequently stumbles. This can often lead to open injuries in the area of the coronet band.

Suitable corrective measures are movements that enable the rider to exert more power with the inside forward-driving leg and the rein that determines the position of the head in order to improve the elevation of the horse and to ride it increasingly up against the outside rein during further training. Exercises such as the shoulder-in, travers, all types of half-pass movements, in particular on circle lines, pirouettes at the walk, half-turns around the haunches, smaller voltes at the canter and larger canter pirouettes have an extremely favourable effect and ensure that the fault is soon eliminated. Until such time, the rider should hold back from riding small pirouettes at competition standard.

Falling-out of the hindquarters and disunited canter

Faulty, and also frequently observed, is the canter pirouette around the middle where the horse falls out with the hindquarters. Here, the turning axis goes vertically through the centre of the horse. The cause is usually an insufficiently effective or incorrectly placed outside rider's leg in conjunction with a strong pull on the inside rein. In order to be able to better check the resulting slinging effect with its centrifugal forces, the horse supports itself by placing the outside hind leg far sideways (straddling) on the ground, which also often causes it to fall into the disunited canter.

This fault will only improve after the rider has learned to bend his horse, to give it the correct head position, collect it, and keep it in front of his legs. Supportive exercises are lateral movements in frequent changes with the shoulder-in, correct reining back and frequent transition into walk or canter from the halt.

Remarks

The correct application of the aids is very important for the successful execution of the canter pirouette. In the case of lazier horses and deep going, it is necessary to perform the half-halts so carefully that enough energy remains for the actual turn and the horse does not begin to hesitate. In contrast, when dealing with a very frisky or nervy horse and hard going, the retaining aids need to be a bit more pronounced and in particular be applied early enough, in favour of a better elevation.

The canter pirouette places particular stress on the tendons, joints, and discs of the horse. Therefore it should only be executed after careful loosening work and overall very sparingly during daily schooling.

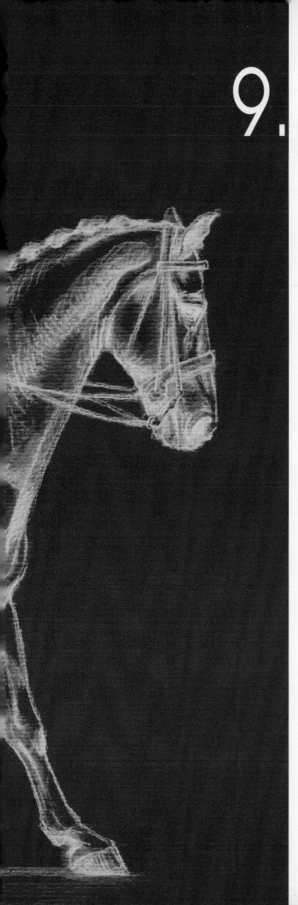

9. Schaukel (Rein-back, Walk Forwards, Rein-back, Walk Forwards)

In the case of the correct execution of the Schaukel, the horse swings its weight increasingly back onto the hindquarters for the rein back and then moves it forwards for the transition to the walk. The observer sees a collected horse, straight in itself which, after a series of half-halts to the halt, walks a certain number of strides backwards with elevation and staying absolutely supple. It then moves smoothly, and without force, into a forward movement at the walk and after a defined number of strides, it changes back smoothly and without stopping into the rein-back. In conclusion it is ridden forwards from this second rein-back at the walk, trot or canter.

The Schaukel serves to further improve the Durchlässigkeit (suppleness) of the already well-trained horse and helps the well-advanced rider to further optimise his already highly sensitive application of the aids. The effect of the Schaukel on the skeleton and muscles is moderate because, at this level of advanced dressage competitions, the trained horse already has the corresponding build-up of muscles. The repeated change of direction within a short space trains the balance however, and the movement has a strong disciplinary value with regard to submission and obedience.

In order for the Schaukel to be successful, the horse needs to remain rounded and supple during the rein-back and in front of the driving aids. Photograph: Bronkhorst

The Schaukel is part of the collective movements and is composed of the trot-like diagonal rein-back, with its two beats and two phases, and of the forward movement of a number of strides at the walk with its four beats and eight phases.

The Schaukel is measured by steps or strides at the walk and rein-back, the number of which can differ depending on the dressage test. Usual requirements are for example 4-4-4 or 4-4-6.

Prerequisites

Prerequisites for the rider

Theoretical foundations

- The rider is well-acquainted with the theory of the progress of the movement, is very responsive, and possesses the necessary sensitivity in order to combine his aids to sequential aid combinations regarding the circumstances.

The seat

- The focal point of the completely engaged dressage seat in this movement is the sufficient erectness of the upright upper body with excellent closure over the shoulders, elbows, and arms to the well carried, closed rider's hands.
- The seat is consolidated in such a way that it can open up immediately from its centre in order to be able to drive the horse forwards with great power.

Prerequisites for the horse

Physiological foundations

- The horse is positioned straight in itself and has an elevated upright neck set firmly at the base so that it allows aids through without any kink or other twists even under the high pressure of collection.
- The well-flexed joints of the hind legs allow the hindquarters to be lowered.

On the aids

- The horse possesses completely consolidated reflexes to forward driving and retaining aids.
- It reacts calmly and without haste and panic to fast aids applied sequentially.
- The necessary co-operation and Durchlässigkeit (suppleness) is reliable and can be asked for at will.

Execution

Preparatory exercises

An indispensable prerequisite for a correctly ridden Schaukel is a horse that stands square. Therefore, repeated half-halts to the halt, frequent transitions to the walk or trot, or rein-back from the halt, form part of the preparatory exercises which can school the horse's obedience regarding the necessary combinations of aids.

Preparation for the movement

The Schaukel can be ridden from the halt on each marker of the school. In competitions, on the other hand, it is demanded either on the centre of the short side or on a point at a ninety degree angle to the centre line – where it can be assessed best by the judges.

After a series of half-halts to the halt, the horse stands square under tension through the flexed joints and remains framed between the aids. The frame is maintained until the horse balances itself and chews on the bit at a good elevation and has the tendency to let the neck drop. The tension and upright carriage in a small space ensure that the horse remains highly sensitive and reactive, so that the rider needs to apply further aids with a great degree of care.

The introductory movement of the horse for the rein-back is similar to that of starting to walk from the halt. Therefore, the rider keeps his legs in front on the girth. From there, he starts driving the horse forwards so carefully that the horse does not get scared but wants to start moving forward slowly. For this purpose it wants to shift its centre of gravity forwards in order to move the leg, as if starting to stride at the walk. One leg is lifted while the others want to push the horse's body forwards.

Shifting the centre of gravity in the direction of motion over the legs, which are still on the ground, is combined with a stretching of the neck which, together with the attempt to move forwards, reaches the bit, held through the rider's well-carried hands. If the rider were to give on the reins now and let the motion out, forwards, the horse could perform the transition to the walk.

In this way however, the pressure on the horse's lower jaw is increased and moves beyond the horse, which is in light contact with the rein, to the extent that the horse is encouraged by the forward-driving rider to move onto the bit. The retaining hands, with elbows close to the rider's side, shoulders back, and a firm seat are maintained until the horse reacts.

The aids

Depending on its sensitivity, soon and certainly no later than half a stride forwards, the horse, will recognise, through the increasing pressure on its lower jaw, that it is not asked to move forwards at the walk, and will push itself off from the bit backwards. To do this, it raises itself more upright and swings its centre of gravity back over the legs that are still on the ground. It then places the first leg it has lifted backwards onto the ground and into the rein-back, instead of forwards into a walk. In this manner the Schaukel always begins with a half-step forwards and a three-quarter-step backwards which, however, is counted as one whole stride.

In order to ensure that, during this highly sensitive moment, the momentum does not die out and the horse, which is pushed together in itself, remains standing, the rider needs to continue to use the driving aids. With his legs in forward-driving position on the girth, he requests the horse to keep on moving. As the aids frame and limit the horse to the front and the sides, it can only execute this motion backwards.

To do this, it supports itself with one diagonal pair of legs on the ground and pushes the motion backward with the respective hind leg until it is retained by the other diagonal pair of legs. This process, during which the hindquarters are lowered significantly and the pushing hind leg is stretched almost to its full extent under the body of the horse, is counted as a stride. Afterwards, the same progress of motion is repeated until the number of strides asked for has been executed.

While the rider's legs ensure that, during any collected forward movement, the hind legs move as close to the front legs as possible, they now also ensure that the hind legs cannot develop a greater scope of motion than the front legs. This is so that the horse cannot fall apart as it goes backwards. The tension from the halt therefore remains unchanged, while the collection can be increased to such a degree that the rider is able to demand a shorter scope of motion with the horse's hind legs than with the front legs. In this manner, the front legs step slightly closer to the hind legs with each stride. However this only happens if the horse remains in front of the forward-driving aids during the entire process.

To break off the backward motion, the rider pushes his hands, which have been retaining the forward momentum, slightly forwards, shortly before the conclusion of the last stride and without tipping forwards with his upper body. Thus the horse is no longer asked to push itself backward but can, instead, move forwards again. In order to ensure that tension and collection are maintained, the rider pushes the horse on with his forward-driving legs to follow the reins. In this manner the horse absorbs the backward motion gently with the hind legs and propels itself forwards – the centre of gravity of the horse swings smoothly forward and the neck is stretched in the direction of motion.

This time, the sensitive, giving rider's hands permit the forward movement and allow the horse a larger frame. The horse fills the frame by stepping forwards purposefully supported by the rider's forward-driving leg aids.

The horse is now in a well collected and controlled walk, in which the rider applies the aids as usual and ensures that the control of the poll, chewing on the bit and Durchlässigkeit (suppleness) are maintained. Due to the high degree of collection, the nodding movement of the horse's neck and head is very limited but needs to be let out by the rein, on the same side, following the swinging motion, to ensure that the horse does not tense up. At the same time the rider counts the strides at the walk in order not to miss the most important phase of the movement. Its exact start is dependent on the sensitivity of the horse, which the rider needs to be able to feel and estimate correctly.

Initially, towards the end of the walk phase, the horse will be ridden into an elevation to the limits of its ability, by means of half-halts, to ensure that it cannot evade the aids with its neck. The hands, which up to this point have let the forward movement of the walk through, are once more carefully taken back into the retaining position. The horse feels as if the bit were coming towards it and will start to decrease the tempo of the forward movement.

Despite this the horse ends up restrained against the bit. The pressure on the lower jaw increases slowly. The remaining forwards movement has enough propulsion and energy left that the rider need only accompany the process with his legs in front on the girth. In this position, they also ensure that the horse cannot evade the increasing pressure, which is building up straight between the hind legs and the bit, by kinking its neck at the base and falling out through one shoulder or the other.

The pressure point of the increasingly pronounced contact with the reins needs to be reached in time with the conclusion of the last stride of the walk, at which the horse wants to relax the contact and the rider needs to work against this from his seat. In the case of well-ridden horses, this pressure point is so pleasantly light that even children without great strength can hold out against it.

The front legs stop, the hind legs keep on moving and increasingly step under the centre of gravity, if they are requested to do so, by the applied forward-driving aids of the rider. If the rider misses this opportunity, the hind legs will stop at the same time as the front legs, the horse comes to a halt and the Schaukel has been executed incorrectly. With the correct aids, the horse pushes itself together, needs to bounce off the bit by shifting its centre of gravity from the front to the back smoothly and without hesitation, and pushes itself off backwards energetically, with hind legs placed far under the body.

In this manner, the horse has swung its movement backwards again. It will immediately start to swing in the two beats and two phases of the rein-back from one diagonal pair of legs to the other, as long as the rider sits quietly and asks it to perform the movement with his forward-driving leg aids at the front on the girth.

Conclusion of the movement

For the conclusion of the movement it is of course important that the Schaukel should end with a transition to the walk, the trot, or the canter. In each case the respective aid is given carefully and without disturbing the remaining process during the last stride of the rein-back. The horse needs to obey the aid after the last stride. At the same time the rider yields the retaining rein aids and allows a wider frame, which the horse fills out through a renewed shifting of its centre of gravity to the front and through the transition into the requested pace.

Evaluation

The Schaukel will tell the expert observer what degree of Durchlässigkeit (suppleness), flexion of the hocks, and collection the horse has achieved and how far the dexterity of the rider's aids has improved. In particular, however, the seat of the rider and its stability can be judged – during the circumstances of the Schaukel they may be tested severely.

Critical moments

During the Schaukel, the horse initially needs to start moving forwards and then after half a stride push itself off backwards against the bit. This moment during which the forwards motion needs to be transformed almost without transition into a backward motion by the horse is one of the most complicated transitions that equitation has to offer, even at the simple rein-back.

It is made distinctly more difficult during the third transition, when the horse needs to change smoothly to a backwards motion from a completed stride forward at the walk, without a halt. This phase is the most complex moment of the exercise.

Accordingly, the preparative exercises need to be thoroughly established so that the horse reacts to the lightest indications of the aids and faults cannot occur in the first place, during this highly sensitive moment.

Achievable degree of skill

The Schaukel is the product of years of often lengthy and strenuous training of rider and horse and is therefore only demanded in advanced dressage competitions in certain countries. The achievable degree of skill can only lie in an improvement of the transitions and of the paces in-between. If the horse has been sufficiently sensitised, it is however suitable as an outstanding preparation for the piaffe.

Faults and corrections

The Schaukel in particular tempts the badly trained rider to work predominantly with his hands and to pull the horse backward with the reins.

The fallacy of the relieving forwards seat with forwards bent upper body which the rider is supposed to adopt to relieve the horse's back for the rein-back is still stubbornly bandied about in badly informed circles. During the constant changes of direction of movement of the Schaukel, the incorrect backwards and forwards tipping of the upper body gives the exercise the appropriate, if misleading name.

Lateral evasion

During the rein-back the horse should push itself off the ground energetically, move the legs back in a straight line, and naturally remain straight in itself at the same time. If the hindquarters swing out laterally, the entire straightness, as an element of the training tree, is lost.

If the horse is positioned against the outside track of the school, the rider gets the feeling of the horse swinging out laterally and in an arc with the inside hind leg – in particular on the right rein, which is the more difficult side for most horses.

This seemingly lateral evasive action, which the inexperienced rider seems to feel, only occurs, however, in the rarest circumstances through the inside hind leg. In most cases, the cause is a kink at the base of the neck or a curvature in the spine. These twists control the hind legs, which are positioned straight in themselves, via the croup and thus gives them the incorrect direction of motion towards the centre of the school. A wheelbarrow is a good illustrative example: its fixed front wheel would run dead straight if left to its own devices, were the user not to turn it in another direction via the handles.

As a corrective measure, the rider should initially not perform the Schaukel and only demand the rein-back from the halt. For this purpose the basic set-up of the horse needs to be checked and corrected until the horse stands evenly on all four legs and straight in itself. Then both the rider's legs need to be in the same position on either side, and give the aid with equal effect, as the back can also be twisted through unevenly applied aids, which then force the hind legs into an incorrect movement via the haunches.

Both reins, which the horse is supposed to push itself backward from, need to be the same length and have the same effect to prevent any kink in the neck. This also controls the hind legs via the haunches and swings them away from the correct direction of motion. The rider needs to sit precisely in the centre of the saddle with his weight evenly distributed on both seat bones – a crooked seat has an enormous influence on the direction of motion.

If the horse still pushes inwards, maybe from force of habit, the rider's leg on the same side needs to be taken back into a restraining position behind the girth, and the horse needs to be bent back with the diagonal leg and rein. In stubborn cases, it is recommended to position the shoulders of the horse slightly into the centre of the school so that it is easier for the horse to move in the direction of the outside track of the school at the moment its leg lifts off the ground. However, corrections, with a leg placed back in a retaining position, are only recommended for horses that hold on to their willingness to move if, in its retaining position behind the girth, the forward-driving impulse of the leg is missing.

There are difficult cases where the rider's retaining leg has to become a laterally acting one. In this case, the horse is reined back on the circle line of a volte, the bend of which is determined by the laterally driving leg. As soon as the corrective measures show signs of success, they can be included into the work during the Schaukel.

Rushing backwards or dropping behind the bit

Horses that rush or crawl back usually remain completely straight in themselves and have developed a different method of fighting against the rider's aids other than through distortion or kinks in the body. Both faults have in common that they demonstrate an incorrect form of motion that can only be corrected through better forward-driving aids of the rider.

As a rule, the horse that rushes backwards, flees from rough rein aids straight between the rider's legs. It thereby positions itself behind the forward-driving aids of the rider's legs and can initially only be stopped and calmed down through the use of energetic forward-driving measures. In order to counteract the bit hurting the mouth, the horse dives down with a long neck, pushes itself off against the reins and escapes explosively with stiff hind legs wide apart and high hindquarters. Only those riders who retain their seat without moving in the saddle during this moment and do not fall forward have any justified chance of being able to correct the fault.

As the front legs move in a similar fashion, the body of the horse wavers from one diagonal to the other so that the rider feels as if he is sitting in a rocking boat, which wants to slip out under him at the front. Due to frequent collisions of the lateral pairs of legs, injuries in the area of the back coronet bands and torn-off shoes on the front hoofs cannot be excluded. Often this rushing backward is accompanied by a tongue over the bit.

Simply throwing away the reins doesn't help in the least. On the contrary; in order to succeed in placing this horse back into a frame and rein it back with the help of all aids in beautiful collection, the horse needs to learn to accept the rein aids and therefore maintain the strong contact. This can only be achieved with energetic forward-driving legs, which may need to be supported emphatically with spurs and schooling whip.

It goes without saying that the rein aids may only be used extremely sensitively, and in a restrained fashion. Calming gestures on the part of the rider need to go far beyond the normal, in order to keep the horse's nerves stable during these corrective measures.

The horse that is dropping behind the bit also lacks the forward-driving impulse. This could have a positive influence on its legs, which are working insufficiently. Often these horses are ridden by riders who pull hard on the reins. They show no elevation, brace themselves against the bit, and only back off unwillingly against the force. In extreme cases, they pull each leg back, almost

If the rider pulls with his hands, the horse will tend to dive down and
evade the backward aids, with stiff hind legs and high hindquarters.

individually, in an irregular sequence of footfalls and leave clear drag marks on the ground.

These horses are usually not on the aids very well in any case, and it makes no sense to arm the rider with spurs or schooling whips. It is better to initially ensure a distinct improvement of the horse chewing on the bit, control of the poll region and Durchlässigkeit (suppleness), so that the horse that is driven forwards and to rein back actually pushes itself backwards off the bit.

A rider who is unable to drive the horse forwards with any purpose can induce a horse to drop behind the bit. As a rule, these are usually weak riders or children who have been taught to use forward-driving aids for the rein-back without monitoring their progress. These riders then sit on rigidly stiff stationary horses and try to get the horse to execute any motion by pulling on the reins and kicking with their legs, using spurs and schooling whip excessively. If the horse eventually executes the much-desired stride backwards the riders, and in some cases also their trainers, feel their actions justified and kick even harder. After a while, the upset horse is too frightened to move in the direction from which the painful aids are coming and remains standing in one place or simply pushes itself and the bit forwards.

The corrective measure is simple. Here, as always, transitions featuring legs crossing over or leg yielding result in the horse learning to better observe the leg aids of the rider. Only then should reining back and the Schaukel be pursued further, before other signs of insubordination creep in.

Hesitant transitions

The well-ridden Schaukel distinguishes itself in the first instance by its flowing transitions that look effortless. Despite this, if one looks closely there is inevitably a moment between the forwards and backward movement during which the horse comes to a standstill, similar to a child's swing. The fine art in the execution of the movement is to keep this moment as short as possible and almost make it disappear. If this is not successful, we talk of hesitant transitions.

Speed is therefore the defining element because naturally there is very little time available for smooth transitions. This is also true for the rider's aids, which can only be the lightest indications of aids. In addition, the respective reaction times of the horse, which needs to remain consistently in the centre of the frame and must not support itself too much on the bit or against the rider's legs, need to be correspondingly short.

As horses do not know how many steps or strides they need to go backwards and forwards, the aids need to be very precise. The horse will feel the aids better and much more sensitively the less they disappear under a plethora of other aids which are necessary to maintain the backwards or forwards movement of horses that are ridden incorrectly.

When schooling the young horse, the trainer should therefore take care that it learns as soon as possible to walk forwards or backwards without the rider's aid. In this way the rider – apart from small corrective measures – only needs to become active with regard to a change of direction of the motion. Light, almost invisible, aids are completely sufficient for this purpose and rough mechanical aids are unnecessary.

As transitions of any kind can lead to a greater sensitivity of the horse, consequently the Schaukel improves this too. In addition, the movement itself, if applied proficiently, can be used to correct inconsistencies in the Durchlässigkeit (suppleness) of the horse.

Incorrect number of steps or strides

Errors in the number of the requested strides or steps usually occur during the rein-back phase – in the majority of cases horses execute more strides than demanded.

In addition to imprecise or even incorrect aids, the cause frequently lies in sudden changes that originate from the horse. A serious problem is the sudden loss of tension in horses that begin to tire, fall apart, and find themselves behind the forward-driving aids. In the same way as with horses which become confused or begin to execute the piaffe, the rider will only be able to save the exercise if the horse has already learned to react to the lightest indications of aids. Even professionally trained riders will only be capable of correcting the outline and tension of the horse during the short time available at the end of a phase with the help of the transition.

In the case of horses that only tend to make mistakes in the number of steps during the execution of the Schaukel, and those who have no problems whatsoever executing the rein-back itself, it helps in most instances to ride a greater number of strides with an increasingly lower number of steps and vice versa. This enables these horses to swing back and forth better, keep their balance and remain in front of driving aids. In this way the Schaukel can be designed variably for practice purposes with sequence patterns of 6-4-6-3-6-2 or 6-4-5-4-3-4 and similar. Several transitions, one after another from the halt to rein-back, with short pauses, may also cure the problem as long as the horse remains in front of the rider's legs.

If a horse has a tendency to start executing the piaffe, it is usually sufficient to reduce the inherent tension to keep it at a collected walk. It makes sense to offer a larger frame during the moment of transition. This ensures that the horse is able to drop its neck further down. Half-halts executed reciprocally on both reins can also be helpful. In order to remove the fault more quickly, the start of the execution of the piaffe from the halt should initially be put aside during schooling sessions, and more should be demanded originating from the forwards momentum.

In order to prevent the horse from starting to trot, which can also occur, an almost contrary reaction is necessary. The rider needs to prevent naturally hasty, too rough, forward-driving aids. In addition, however, the frame into which a horse falls to trot is too large because it does not offer sufficient support for the collected walk. Out of fear of further strides at the trot, inexperienced riders have a tendency to drive the horse forwards insufficiently or not at all during the transition from rein-back to walk. By doing this they apply completely wrong measures of correction. After all, the cause is not the intense forward motion of the hind leg from the back to the front, but its control. The problem is usually solved if the rider only moves the hands forwards after the lift-off of the hind leg and without interruption of connection to the horse's mouth.

Hindquarters slipping under the body

Slippery surfaces or horse shoes are not always to blame when the horse's hind legs slip underneath the torso during the transition from the forwards to the backwards movement. Often the fault lies in a rough rider's grip which pulls up the horse's neck abruptly at the front so that the back of the horse is lowered, this in turn affects the hind legs. As this causes significant pain, the horse

A rider's rough grip, which pulls the horse's head upwards, leads to tensing up in the horse's back, and the hind legs slip under the body out of control.

tenses up and remains stiff in the hind legs, which then slip away out of control underneath its body.

In the long run, this kind of transition will not only lead to considerable damage to the spinal column but also to disobedient horses that increasingly refuse to step under their centre of gravity at all due to a mounting fear of pain. Eventually, such horses will only be able to execute a completely tense stepping on the spot instead of a flowing transition,

until they finally find the correct direction of motion backwards, which they subsequently throw themselves into.

Other faults will follow if the rider now tries to drive the horse's hind legs, which are stretched back for a good reason, under the centre of gravity by force, or even tries to transform the stamping into a piaffe.

The owners of such horses should give the riders a stern warning or stop them from riding the horse entirely before the horse's trust in a rider has been lost completely and irreparable damages in the area of the spinal column leads to expensive veterinary bills. Riders who want to correct such horses need to put aside the execution of the Schaukel until the trust of the horse has been re-established by means of carefully introduced sequences of half-halts to the halt.

Remarks

Due to its advanced requirements regarding the sensitivity of the seat and aids of the rider, the Schaukel separates the wheat from the chaff, and not only at competitions.

In addition, there are only a few movements where the rider is dependent on the co-operation of the horse to the same degree as in the Schaukel. As the phases of this exercise flow into each other, almost without introduction, and the high quality of each one is decisive for the execution of the other, the horse has, in principle, plenty of opportunities to express its irritation. In addition, rider and horse need to cope with the completely different foot-falls in opposite directions of motion, which lead to an extraordinary stress on the haunches.

This knowledge regarding the complexity of the exercise should be an occasion for some riders to view their horse with more humbleness, gratitude and respect.

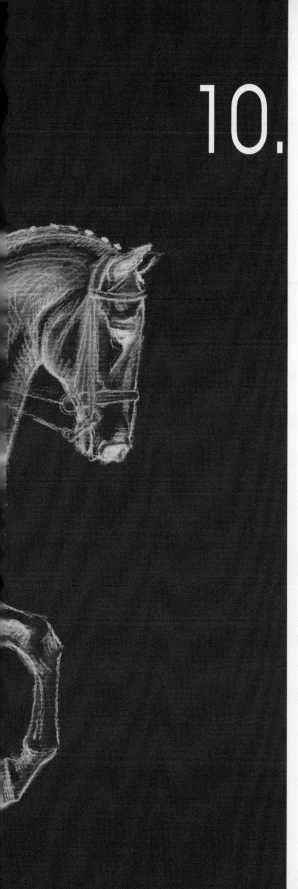

10. Piaffe

If the piaffe is executed correctly the observer will see a highly elevated horse that is straight in itself, with distinctly recognisable forward motion, in a trot-like movement on the spot. The back muscles are flexing elastically and, the lowered hindquarters have simultaneously taken up the weight, and the hocks are increasingly flexed. At the same time, the hoofs of the hind legs are lifted of the ground energetically, to the level of the fetlock joints.

The horse lifts its forearms almost to the horizontal and then places them on the ground vertically. There is a short pause during the phase of suspension between the grounding of each diagonal pair of legs in the distinct two-beat.

The piaffe leads the horse to the top level of its ability to collect itself and further perfects the Durchlässigkeit (suppleness) of the rein and leg aids, which are working together. Due to the work on a very small space with a minimal phase of suspension and a limited pushing force in favour of the load-bearing capacity of the hindquarters, it further schools the horse's feeling of balance.

During the piaffe, the hindquarters need to take up a maximum amount of weight and the horse thereby flexes increasingly in the hocks. Depending on the degree of collection this leads to a distinct build-up of strength and muscles, and to changes of the muscle tone in the area of the hindquarters, back, trapezius and upper neck line.

This is the only way in which the forehand can be relieved to enable the horse to lift its forearms as horizontally as possible. The muscle groups, tendons, ligaments and joints in the chest, shoulders and forelegs are also distinctly strengthened and positively influenced in their free progress of motion.

The piaffe belongs to a group of highly collective lessons and may initially remind the observer of the trot, due to the progress of motion with the sequence of footfalls of the diagonal pairs of legs. However, while the trot progresses in two beats and three phases, during the piaffe the horse moves in two beats and two phases in a similar way to the rein-back. Due to the almost complete lack of the phase of suspension, the movement can therefore only be referred to as similar to the trot.

During the piaffe, the horse steps with diagonal pairs of legs without gaining space forwards and takes up an increasing amount of weight with the hindquarters. The forearm is lifted almost to the horizontal. Photograph: Schnitzer

The length of the piaffe is measured in strides, which are counted in the same way as strides at the trot. It is the only movement during which the forward striding extension is positively limited. As a rule, two hooves' widths are allowed, in a few dressage tests it is a metre.

Owing to the lack of space covered, the piaffe is classically suited for good preparation via work from the ground, or between pillars, and thus to introduce it safely to young riders and horses. Furthermore, it forms the initial basis for many airs above the ground (Haute École), such as are perfectly displayed in the Spanish Riding School in Vienna or in the Cadre Noir in the French town of Saumur.

Prerequisites

Prerequisites for the rider

Theoretical foundations

- The rider is well-acquainted with the theoretical foundations of the movement, possesses a good responsiveness, and is competent enough to adapt his aids to the reactions of the horse and to combine them in a fast, sequential order and fine-tuned combination.
- The rider, with his well-developed sensitivity of the seat, is able to perfectly differentiate between the phases of the placing on and lifting off the ground of the horse's legs.

The seat

- The rider securely masters the completely engaged dressage seat. A focal point of this is the correct erectness of the upright upper body with excellent closure over the shoulders, elbows and arms to the well-carried, closed rider's hands.
- From the centre of the saddle, the rider is capable of quickly opening up if necessary from his supple position in order to be able to drive the horse strongly forwards.

Prerequisites for the horse

Physiological foundations

- Even at a high degree of collection the horse remains straight in itself.
- The neck can be steady on the base and can be brought to a good elevated position.
- The flexibility in the mouth and poll results from a good chewing on the bit and the joints of the hind legs are highly supple and flexible because they have been required to step under the body consistently during the preceding collective work in all paces.

On the aids

- The horse reacts in a consolidated way to forward-driving and retaining aids and has the necessary composure to understand and act upon a rapid sequence of aids without haste and panic.
- The willingness to co-operate and a high degree of Durchlässigkeit (suppleness) need to be available even when a schooling whip is to be used for the support of the forward-driving aids.

In the case of this piaffe from the ground, the energetic lifting-off of the hind legs to the level of the fetlock joints is well developed. Photograph: Horses in Media/Guni

Execution

Preparatory exercises

Quite apart from such valuable movements as the halt, the rein-back, and the Schaukel, which can also lead directly to the piaffe, work in-hand or between the pillars is the most careful way to develop the piaffe. It is also the method that offers the greatest degree of success for horse and rider. While only a few riding institutes provide pillars, almost every well-managed riding school will have reins for work from the ground, or lungeing reins, lungeing girths, side reins, and lungeing cavessons.

It is now possible to divide the training of the suitably tacked-up horse, which is made to stand close to the outside track of the school, into separate phases.

First phase: Due to careful use of the in-hand whip and a soft, leading, lungeing hand the horse is familiarised with the collaboration of the forward-driving and retaining aids, working in-hand from the ground.

Second phase: After this first phase of familiarisation, the horse is encouraged, with the schooling whip and voice, to start trotting with slightly more pronounced aids after which it is brought back to a halt.

Third phase: As soon as the completion of the in-hand strides at the trot have been executed satisfactorily, the horse is asked to collect itself more and more, so that the piaffe-like movements, with a pronounced forwards motion, are developed bit by bit from shortened strides at the trot.

Fourth phase: Once the horse has achieved a high level of collection, and these half strides have been consolidated to such a degree that they essentially correspond to the named characteristics of a piaffe, the scope of motion can slowly be shortened further so that the horse performs a few strides at the piaffe almost on the spot.

Fifth phase: The horse which executes the piaffe in-hand, to a large extent on the spot, can now be burdened with an experienced rider who has a quiet seat, so that the muscles and flexion of the hocks can be further trained evenly on both hands under the rider's weight.

Sixth phase: The trainer on the ground moves increasingly into the background. His application of the aids is gradually replaced by the aids of the rider until the rider eventually takes over sole control of the horse within the course of the last phase.

Preparation for the movement

The piaffe is best developed under the saddle via half strides from the collected walk or from the halt. In the case of advanced schooled horses that are very pliable to the aids, the transition from collected trot to the piaffe can be of greater advantage.

During daily schooling, the legs of the rider have gained the horse's respect, if necessary through energetic use, and the concentrating horse has let them through to such an extent that even the lightest indications of aids suffice in order to immediately trigger the necessary lift-off. In other words, the horse allows itself to be driven forwards and remains steadily in front of the aids.

The horse that is prepared in this manner will now either be standing in a well rounded position at the halt and kept under tension or collected to a high degree once more at the walk and placed in an elevated position. Further half-halts ensure chewing on the bit and control of the poll so that the rider can carry his hands with a light, even contact without the horse changing in itself.

Now the horse is precisely between the aids in the centre of its frame, which is defined and supervised by the rider. The rider sits in a relaxed manner, quietly, and almost passively, with legs touching lightly, well carried hands, and the length of rein matching the good elevation of the horse's neck.

The aids

The rider braces the upper body, relaxes the knee, and starts driving the horse forwards by closing his legs. The highly attentive horse pushes its centre of gravity forwards and raises itself off the ground without delay, through a stretching movement of the hind leg, flexed through the collection at the halt or walk, for its first lift-off. In its conclusion, this action would lead to the free phase of suspension of a normal movement at the trot.

Before the forwards stretching movement of the hind legs, and the pushing force that is directly connected, reach their peak and the horse loses contact with the ground during the phase of suspension, as is usual at the trot, frequent half-halts on the diagonal restrain the forward propulsion. Therefore, the horse's legs remain on the ground; the horse is supported on a diagonal pair of legs so that the phase of suspension that would be the second of the three trotting phases is almost completely omitted. The horse performs a half stride.

The rider's legs continue to request the horse to move forwards. As the horse only has the other diagonal pair of legs, currently lifted off the ground and not supporting the horse, available, it will touch down on the ground with this pair in order to propel itself upwards from the ground again into the phase of suspension. As this intention is prevented anew through effective half-halts from the rider, this phase of suspension is also eliminated. The result is a further half stride.

Due to the fact that the phase of suspension is omitted and the propulsive force is not allowed forwards into the extension of a proper stride at the trot, stretching movement of the hindlegs is limited. This happens to such a degree that the horse is only able to execute on the spot the movement demanded by the rider. In view of the lack of range of motion in the small space allowed, the excess propulsive energy needs to be directed by the horse in the only direction still available, namely underneath the body of the horse and upward. The hind leg therefore swings forwards and upward under the centre of gravity, while the diagonal foreleg is pulled upwards vertically until the forearm has almost reached the horizontal.

As the horse barely moves from the spot during this phase, the front leg is subsequently placed vertically back into the old position – the desired execution of the piaffe is fulfilled. These stages of movement are repeated until the desired number of strides has been completed. In the case of correct execution, the rider has the feeling that the horse is working with all four legs close together on the smallest space possible. The horse becomes larger and lighter in front, while it lowers itself increasingly in the hindquarters to the extent to which the load-bearing capacity of the hind legs has been developed.

Even horses with fast moving legs need a certain amount of time for each cycle of motion. Thereby, while the hind leg of a diagonal touches the ground, takes up weight, and flexes in the joints, the other hind leg needs to bridge the same space of time during the much easier motion upwards. This results in the required delayed moment of suspension of the diagonal pair of legs that are not on the ground.

Potential differences between horse and rider can initially occur because inexperienced horses, depending on their temperament, will want to push out forwards from the frame designated to them, or will not want to move at all, and will require a flexible adaptation of the applied aids. Depending on possibly very fast-changing conditions, the half-halt will initially need to dominate during one stride, and then the forward-driving leg aid, until the horse is once more in balance in the centre of its frame and starts to piaffe independently, and with regularity.

The goal is a rhythmic, diagonally alternating, energetic lifting off and touching down on the ground with both diagonal pairs of legs, which work with increased energy on the spot because of the limited spatial scope. In the case of a fully trained horse, the overall length travelled forwards will only be one or two hooves' widths within one entire piaffe cycle.

This basic form of the piaffe, offered by the horse itself, allows the rider to blend more and more into the background where he only needs to see to an improved execution of the movement with even lighter aids. To achieve this improvement the horse needs to push itself together and collect itself even further. It thus becomes broader in its torso, which swings from side to side in rhythm with the alternately stepping diagonal pairs of legs. This swinging motion magically draws the loosely placed rider's legs to the horse's side and they swing rhythmically along the horse's body so that during the moment of lift-off, during which the leg drives the horse forward, the aid is applied almost automatically. So basically, the horse picks up its impulsion by itself.

Conclusion of the movement

The different combinations of aids which can be applied to conclude the piaffe are determined by whether the horse subsequently comes to a halt, walks on, or is supposed to do the transition to the passage.

In order to come to a halt, the rider no longer asks for motion but through suitable half-halts keeps the horse rounded, and loose, and on the bit with a relaxed poll. As a rule, the motion then stops immediately.

In order to complete the transition to a walk, it is sufficient in most cases to extend the frame by lengthening the reins and giving with both hands to such an extent that the horse can stretch itself. As a rule, the inherent, strenuous tension and acute collection of the piaffe collapses very quickly, which most horses demonstrate by moving off in a relaxed walk. The rider needs to be sure to follow the nodding movement of the horse's head with his hands.

For the transition to the passage, it will initially be necessary to extend the frame to such an extent that the horse can push itself off again into the free phase of suspension, with the rider's legs asking for the additional forward movement. The phase of suspension is then shortened through corresponding rein aids in such a way that the horse will push itself off in an increasingly upward direction.

Evaluation

The piaffe gives the expert observer an idea about the degree of achievable collection and the attained feeling of balance of the horse shown. It demonstrates clearly to what extent the haunches are capable of taking up the weight, gives inferences regarding the aptitude of the horse for advanced dressage through the extent of the lifting motion of the forearms, and gives indications regarding the precision of the rider's aids.

Critical moments

As in the case of many collective exercises, the critical phase of the piaffe is the moment during which the forward-driving aids have an effect on the retaining ones. The moment, in other words, during which the horse needs to push itself together and at the same time is expected to keep on striding with its legs.

While the competition rider naturally has no choice at which point he demands the horse to perform the piaffe during the dressage test, he should adapt the daily schooling session to the psychological state of the horse. He should also take into account the horse's form on the day when he introduces the first strides at the piaffe.

Energetic horses with sensitive mouths and good Durchlässigkeit (suppleness) will find it easier to initially move into the piaffe from the collected trot. However, those which need a lot of forward impulsion, and which are equipped with rubbery, less sensitive mouths, are more likely to develop the piaffe from the halt or via the collected walk.

Achievable degree of skill

The piaffe is one of the few movements for which the achievable degree of skill is dependent on the further intended purpose of the horse. While riders of the Haute École search for the achievable degree of skill in a levade and other airs above the ground, riders who prefer to remain on the ground will be satisfied with a piaffe that has been developed to perfection and which, due to its gymnastic effect, contributes towards the horse remaining supple and rideable into old age.

Faults and corrections

Due to the fact that in the eyes of many inexperienced riders the piaffe is simply a trampling movement on the spot, many indoor and outdoor schools experience virtual dramas when this movement is performed. While some horses can be talked into executing a few helpless motions with the aid of long schooling whips and spurs, many of these poor animals do not allow the correct movement to be a subsequent formed, due to a lack of Durchlässigkeit (suppleness). Unfortunately, we therefore frequently observe riders who pull and yank on the reins and who try to apply the aids in the roughest manner and with the help of artificial means. They turn out completely distressed horses that stop at some stage and are then given a solid beating before, after weeks of martyrdom, they begin to fight against their "riders".

Some pull out all the stops of their strength and they bolt or they rear so that they become a danger to life and limb of all those involved, until they have nothing left to give. Others, often the more sensitive horses, will limit themselves to resistance of a more subtle kind. They start with distortion and twisting of all kinds down to the tongue over the bit, crunching of the teeth, and similar measures during which they trample around on the spot and give the rider the much desired movement on the spot, which he gratefully misinterprets as a piaffe.

Whichever fault remains at the conclusion of such mis-spent schooling, any such riding will never lead to a perfect piaffe, which trains and exercises the horse and can develop it to the highest level. This alone, however, is the purpose of the movement.

Rearing

The piaffe under the rider also belongs to the movements of the Haute École and is amongst other things the basic exercise for the levade which is developed from it with the aid of a schooling half-halt. The experienced judge and rider who has understood these interconnections, will thereby only judge such piaffes as well executed when he can imagine them as a preliminary stage for the levade.

The horse places the inside hind leg forwards, under the centre of gravity, as required for the airs above the ground, from a number of energetic strides at the piaffe. If the horse does not flex its haunches under its weight and does not lower its hindquarters but instead pushes itself up with stiff hind leg joints, it will rear as a result.

A rearing horse is usually produced by a rider who tries to get motion from the horse by force, and at the same time restricts the horse with sharp artificial aids. The horse, which in its desperation looks for a way out, finds its way backwards and forwards blocked off through the whip and bit. The next alternative is the way upwards and he realises that all pain stops in that position, and even the most forceful rider suddenly clings to the horse's neck in a very subdued manner.

This helps the horse to decide that he should do this sooner and more often in future, as it saves it a lot of work and pain. It is not uncommon for both horse and rider to suffer severe injuries having fallen over backwards.

The trainer who has to correct such a horse has a difficult task at hand. Initially it is important to find out why the horse rears. If it rears only from fear and bad experiences, trust-building measures which offer the horse rewards and success experiences, and excluding the piaffe from the schooling sessions, can help cure this trait. Great patience and time are required. However, pain in the area of the thoracic vertebrae and in the back muscles can also be the reason for rearing. The rider needs initially to find out if that is the case and if necessary introduce the appropriate treatment before a new approach via half strides can lead to success.

Above the rein

During the piaffe, the horse has a high degree of elevation. Its highest point of the neck is the poll, between the atlas and the axis. The line from the forelock down the nose remains slightly in front of the vertical.

A horse that is in front of the bit can also fulfil the criteria of the outside shape of the horse. It also presents a very high elevation and has the nose in front of the vertical. For the experienced observer, however, that is where the similarities with a well-ridden horse on the bit and aids end. While the latter pushes its propulsive energy via a relaxed back forwards onto the bit, where it can be transformed if the horse willingly gives in the poll, the former stiffens in the back and pushes itself up in front.

In this case, the line of the nose of such horses doesn't always give a clear indication – it suffices if the horse simply blocks in the poll region. The unnaturally highly elevated neck is supported in this position by well-developed muscles of the lower part of the neck until the neck in its convex bend looks like a giraffe's neck. This ewe neck has a lever-like effect on the hind legs, via the stiff and unyielding back. The hind legs subsequently flex too far or push stiff-legged against the created motion energy.

If the hind legs flex too far, step under the horse's body, and take up weight, they are unable to push this weight forwards any longer so that any forwards motion is lost and the horse cannot develop a stable contact with the reins. The hind legs seem to be glued to the ground and seem to want to crawl further and further under the horse's body, while the forelegs no longer fulfil their role in a support function. They often lose their contact to the ground and almost seem to tumble around freely in the air. As such horses become tired very quickly they start supporting the movements with a nodding motion of the head which is reminiscent of hens pecking for food.

If, on the other hand, the hindquarters of a horse remain stiff, the exact opposite happens. The hind legs push forwards far too strongly, the rider cannot settle down in the saddle and is constantly required to either keep the stiff hind legs in motion or to restrain the forwards propelling motion. This causes the horse to tense up even further. Therefore, the rider sits restlessly and loosely, keeps on bouncing in the saddle, and is incapable of applying correct and precise aids. That is another reason why the horse does not enter into a small frame in the centre of the aids, does not push itself together correctly, and cannot work in collection in a small space.

In both cases, which also often come with a tongue over the bit, the corrective measure needs to be to emphatically drive the horse forwards. Only in a very few exceptional cases will it be possible to almost eliminate the problems quickly merely by applying a few energetically forward-driving measures. This is because as a rule these horses have been asked too early, and over a lengthy period of time, to plod around on the spot at the price of a secure forward motion, rein contact, and chewing on the bit. Therefore, initially the horses need to be brought on the bit in order to learn to accept it again. It goes without saying that, in the event of resistance on the part of the horse, the rider's hands may only be applied in a very careful manner in order not to frighten the horse, which will initially only step forwards hesitantly.

In order to further facilitate the corrective measure for the horse, a great number of gentle, drawn-out transitions between the collected trot and the piaffe offer more help than hours of piaffe cycles.

Lack of regularity

The good piaffe captivates not only through the regulated, mechanically perfect work of the front legs, but also particularly through the energetic, rhythmic lifting off from and touching down on the ground of the hind legs.

In order to perfect the movement, which the horse demonstrates naturally and independently in the wild, the horse needs to work independently during this exercise, carry itself, and give the rider only little occasion to interfere in the process of the motion through

Irregularities in the rein contact – here the distortion in the poll – lead to lack of regularity at the piaffe. The rhythmic lifting off from and touching down on the ground of the hind legs is disturbed significantly.

application of the aids. All distortions, tension and other types of resistance will inevitably lead to motion disturbances and thereby also cause lack of regularity.

Irregularities in the application of the aids, weight distribution, and rein contact can also disturb the rhythm – as can a badly fitted saddle or bit as they usually influence the motion processes, which are normally the same on both sides, differently. The "piaffes" are particularly susceptible to lack of regularity when a rider incessantly kicks and hits his horse with short spurs and a short schooling whip. This he does while he clings by the reins to the horse's mouth, which is fitted with a rubber (gentle) bit, and thinks he is training the horse to the most advanced levels in a "loving and considerate way".

In this situation the basic problem is usually the rider's application of the aids, which fail to motivate the horse to co-operate willingly, are not effective enough, and which therefore need to be constantly repeated. In most cases a single clear tap with the whip or half-halt on the rein would be sufficient to conclude the unsuccessful daily confrontations, which often continue for years, and instead produce a horse which can work independently and without being disturbed. Unfortunately this corrective measure is, as a rule, rejected by this type of "caring" rider as being too rough – this naturally means that even the best trainer is doomed to remain unsuccessful.

Swaying piaffe

In executing the piaffe the horse works in a very small and narrow space. This not only requires a well-defined feeling of balance, but also a high level of trust in a rider who sits absolutely evenly and quietly. Additionally, it requires the secure Durchlässigkeit (suppleness) in the poll which allows the horse to push the motion of the front and hind legs forwards in line and on narrow tracks, because it meets no resistance apart from the half-halts, which merely suppress the phase of suspension.

Apart from a few horses that have managed to reach this level of dressage despite conformation faults, such as hind legs that are too steeply inclined and other limitations, and which can only perform the piaffe with a slight swaying motion due to anatomical reasons, this fault is generally a sign of defects in the schooling. The motion created by the hind legs cannot flow unimpeded through the horse and pass out at the front through the mouth in the case of a relaxed poll, due to resistance of all kinds, ranging from distortion in the neck to tongue over the bit. Instead it remains stuck somewhere along the line, most usually in the neck area. The horse does not push itself together or collect itself, but instead evades the aids with its sideways motion.

So that the horse can support its movements, which increasingly sway laterally, it will now start to place its legs wider and wider apart. In order to be able to push its own body weight, as well as that of the rider, from one side to the other without elasticity, the front legs in particular are spread wide apart and the joints of the hind legs are stretched and connected via a stiff back. To ensure that the swaying structure does not collapse, head and neck serve as a counter balance and usually sway close to the ground in the opposite direction. Only completely inexperienced judges and riders confuse such forms of motion, which are more reminiscent of the "nodding dog" on the parcel shelf of a saloon car, with a piaffe.

The appropriate corrective measures follow logically from the description of the fault. The motion of the horse needs to be directed forwards again through energetic forward-driving measures. At this point, however, they need to meet a distinctly improved Durchlässigkeit (suppleness) of the entire neck formation that will allow the motion to pass through to the bit. The rein needs to release the movement correspondingly, so that it does not remain stuck again. The rein-back or the Schaukel are, for example, supporting exercises which eliminate existing resistance and tension if they are applied correctly.

Too much forward movement

Despite the demanded, recognisable forward motion, a forward movement of only one to two hooves' width overall (although in certain dressage tests it can be an entire metre) is permissible in the piaffe. This is achieved through the elimination of the phase of suspension, with the aid of which the horse otherwise covers much ground at the trot. But even without the moment of the phase of suspension, which turns the strides at the trot into half strides, the horse still has some motion forwards which would overstep the permitted space travelled forward in the piaffe by quite a length. Only by ensuring that the hind legs step well under the body and by collecting the horse can the rider reduce this forwards motion further to meet the conditions for the piaffe.

This, in other words, means that horses which move too far forwards have stagnated halfway through their schooling, because hindquarters which take up weight and are flexed in their joints, as the correctly executed piaffe demands, should not after all be capable of a greater forwards extending motion. It is this forwards extending motion, however, which is responsible for the horse moving too far forwards.

Here again, it is possible that a lack of Durchlässigkeit (suppleness) restricts the rider from shortening the inherent existing motion to such an extent that the horse pushes itself together, collects itself, and takes up weight with its hind legs.

The frequent execution of the piaffe from the halt can support the rider in his efforts to transform the half strides into piaffe strides. This can be done without spoiling the horse's pleasure in moving, as, in contrast to the walk or the collected trot, the halt does not build a foundation on which the horse can stretch and extend itself.

Sticky hind legs

The horse should demonstrate very short moments of suspension in between each of the diagonal pairs of legs touching the ground in the clear two-beat motion which gives the piaffe its dynamic expression. On the other hand, horses with sticky hind legs practically seem to stick to the ground, as the name suggests. The motion of the hind legs is usually limited to a repeated short casual giving way, or flexing, in the joints which does not, however, provide for any forwards motion whatsoever.

The outward image of such sticky hind legs is similar in many horses – entirely different to that of the many different correlated types of faults of movement of the forehand. Anything can be observed here, ranging from laterally swinging forelegs through those which no longer move at all, to movements which show almost arrhythmic characteristics and which are completely independent to each sequence of footfalls.

To start off with, there may be health reasons that make it impossible for the horse to lift the hind legs from the ground. There may be damage to the spine, which includes kissing spines, where the neural spines of the thoracic vertebrae knock together painfully, or there may be degenerative changes to the cruciate ligaments and hocks, the flexibility of which are restricted significantly through the so-called spavin. Apart from that, however, if the horse with sticky hind legs lacks any dynamic in the hind legs during the piaffe, the fault again usually lies predominantly in errors made during the schooling process. Usually the horses affected are those which try to evade stepping up to the bit in order not to be confronted with sharp bits or rough rider's hands, or to run into draw reins and other artificial rein aids, which can lead to them becoming too tight. As long as they lift up their head or tuck it in, they can also cultivate the stiff poll, the tongue over the bit, or similar faults and thus retain the potential for possible rearing in the future.

Only extremely experienced riders will be able to eliminate the faults exhibited during the piaffe itself, through energetic forward-driving measures together with the necessary rein aids. In this way they ensure that the movements of the hind legs are in harmony with those of the front legs again, that the horse remains straight in itself, and allows the aids from behind to pass through to the front and vice versa. Only when these prerequisites are fulfilled and the horse works in a correct outline will it be possible to develop the healthy tension between the hind legs and the hands that is able to close and collect the horse and let it work independently.

Remarks

Due to the enormous degree of collection required for the piaffe, horses push themselves together longitudinally and inevitably become broader at the same time. This should be taken into account when tightening the girth. Quite often a saddle girth that is too tight prevents good schooling results because it constricts the horse and impairs its breathing.

During the passage, the horse bounces energetically upwards from the ground with the help of its flexed hocks. The forearms are raised up to the horizontal; the movement becomes distinctly elevated and distinguished. Photograph: Stroscher

Although the piaffe should be the result of consistent schooling over many years, which only a few well-trained and experienced trainers are really capable of, it seems to degenerate more and more into a status symbol for many riders. Sadly, abuse such as work with two dressage whips in the hands of children, or "in-hand work" using the entire stable personnel – just to quote two examples – can be observed as the norm in many riding schools. The goal here is to do some radical rethinking, to put in place a critical observation of one's own ability, and not to raise one's profile at the cost of the horse.

11. Passage

If the passage is executed correctly, the observer will see a horse with a high elevation moving in an elevated trotting motion. The pairs of legs that push energetically off the ground in the sequence of footfalls of the trot, lengthen the phase of suspension while gaining little ground. The forearms of the front legs are raised horizontally for this purpose. The hind legs, which are placed well under the body with flexed hocks, bounce the weight straight forwards and upwards energetically and with rhythm.

The passage serves to enable the horse to collect itself at the trot to the utmost of its ability and also to add cadence, as well as to perfect the Durchlässigkeit (suppleness) of the rein and leg aids working together. During the passage the hindquarters not only have to take on a great amount of weight but also have to subsequently "catapult" that weight upwards again. The horse flexes and stretches itself increasingly in the hocks. Depending on the degree of collection, this leads to pronounced growth in strength and musculature in the region of the hindquarters, the back, the trapezius and the top line of the neck.

The active hind legs relieve the forehand and the horse is thus able to lift the forearms up to the horizontal. The muscle groups, tendons, ligaments and joints in the area

During the passage, the horse bounces energetically upwards from the ground with the help of its flexed hocks. The forearms are raised up to the horizontal; the movement becomes distinctly elevated and distinguished. Photograph: Stroscher

of the chest, shoulders and forelegs are also put under a high level of strain, especially as the load carried by the front legs during this movement goes far beyond their normal support function.

The passage is probably the most demanding movement of so-called "General Equitation". While the airs above the ground follow on after the passage in riding institutes such as the Spanish Riding School in Vienna, for the competition rider the scale of movements ends here.

Prerequisites

Prerequisites for the rider

Theoretical foundations

- The rider is well-acquainted with the theoretical foundations of the movement, possesses a good responsiveness and is competent enough to adapt his aids to the reactions of the horse and to combine them in a fast sequential order and fine-tuned combination.
- The rider, with his well-developed sensitivity in the seat, is able to perfectly differentiate between the phases of the placing on and lifting off the ground of the horse's legs.

The seat

- The rider securely masters the completely engaged dressage seat. A focal point of this is the sufficient erectness of the upright upper body with excellent closure over the shoulders, elbows and arms to the well-carried, closed rider's hands.

- From the centre of the saddle, the rider is capable of quickly opening up from his supple central position, if necessary, in order to be able to drive the horse strongly forwards.

Prerequisites for the horse

Physiological foundations

- The horse remains absolutely straight in itself under all circumstances.
- The neck can be steady on the base and can be brought to a good elevated position.
- The flexibility in the mouth and poll results from a good chewing on the bit, and the joints of the hind legs are highly supple and flexible because they have been required to step under the body consistently during the preceding collective work in all paces.

On the aids

- The horse reacts in a consolidated way to forward-driving and retaining aids and has the necessary composure to understand and act upon a rapid sequence of aids without haste and panic.
- A willingness to co-operate and a high degree of Durchlässigkeit (suppleness) need to be available even when a schooling whip is to be used for the support of the forward-driving aids.

Execution

Preparatory exercises

The passage can be seen as a mixture of piaffe and extended trot. Flexibility, the ability to stretch as well as thrust, and the load-bearing capacity of the hind legs need to be equally well developed. It is the function of the half-halts to redirect the thrust, which is developed by the forward-driving aids upwards into the correct direction. In order to achieve this and to be able to incorporate it into the passage, all exercises that perfect the reaction of the horse to these aids are suitable.

Preparation for the movement

In competitions, the passage is frequently ridden between the points D and G on the centre line, in association with piaffe cycles arranged before and after the passage. It can also be demanded on any other track from the medium trot, the collected walk or trot, or from the piaffe and may be concluded similar to the Schaukel through a transition to the canter.

Irrespective of the preceding pace, exercise, or school line, the rider's legs, in the forward-driving position at the front on the girth, have gained the horse's respect, if necessary through energetic use during daily schooling and, in particular, directly before the transition to the passage. The horse is concentrating and lets the aids through to such an extent that even the lightest indications are sufficient to immediately trigger the necessary first stride of the passage. In other words, the horse allows itself to be driven forwards and remains steadily in front of the aids.

The horse will now be kept under tension, and is further elevated and collected. Continuing half-halts ensure chewing on the bit and control of the poll so that the rider can carry his hands with a light, even contact before the transition. Now the horse is precisely between the aids in the centre of its frame, which is defined and supervised by the rider. The rider is sitting in a relaxed manner, quietly and almost passively with lightly touching legs, well carried hands, and the length of rein matching the good elevation of the horse's neck.

The aids

The rider braces the upper body, relaxes the knee and starts driving the horse forwards with his seat and legs during the stretching and thrusting phase of a hind leg. Although the forward-driving aids should not be applied too abruptly, in their form and strength they need to remind the horse very much of the aids for the extended trot.

The horse, concentrating deeply, consequently pushes its centre of gravity forwards and immediately powerfully pushes itself off the ground for the first stride, through a stretching motion of the hitherto collectedly flexed hind leg, which leads in its conclusion to the free phase of suspension.

In the phase of suspension at the extended trot, the horse essentially demonstrates a long, shallow arc during the free flight over the ground. This phase of suspension at the trot and at the canter not only forms the conclusion of the respective sequence of footfalls, but also gives the horse the opportunity to flex the hind legs which have been stretched backwards, bringing them to the front and allowing the horse to land on them. Subsequently it repeats the sequence of footfalls from the beginning.

During the passage the horse should move at a more elevated level, in other words, not so close to the ground – the "flight curve" should adopt another shape. It must not follow forwards in the shallow shape as during the trot, but needs to be positioned shorter and inclined instead more sharply upwards, while the time of the phase of suspension does not necessarily change.

In order, therefore, to change the direction of movement of the horse so that it resembles a higher arc, the rider initially braces the upper body so that the hands receive the required counter force from the seat. With suitable half-halts, the horse's carriage is elevated to the limit of its natural capability and the horse is thus pushed upwards by the thrust caused by the lift-off. To ensure that the horse does not collapse, sink back into the ground, and maybe come to a halt, the rider drives it forwards decisively. Framed between the driving hind legs and the short-time pressure of the bit, the only way that remains for the horse is upward.

This motion upwards is not always very simple, even for well-seated, experienced riders. For one, the rider needs to drive forwards from his seat and offer the necessary stability to the hands with the upper body. On the other hand, however, he needs to yield in the relaxed, supple lumbar region in order not to hinder the upward motion of the horse. It requires some training to follow this high wave motion without leaving the saddle, despite all the tension.

Thus the horse pushes itself upwards off the ground and drops back to the ground after a short but high-arced "flight curve". Here it lands on the other diagonal pair of legs. This moment of the phase of suspension, in which no rider's aids are necessary, offers experienced riders the opportunity to relax, to stretch themselves and to give with the hands until the horse has reached the ground.

Under the pressure of landing, the hind leg underneath the centre of gravity flexes deeply in the joints, while the predominantly non-flexed front leg is only able to yield in the area of the fetlock and the shoulder. The hocks flex and thereby acquire the necessary tension to push the weight of horse and rider upward again with impulsion. The rider drives the horse forwards again thus delivering the impulse necessary for this and subsequently needs to redirect the thrust upward again with the aid of half-halts. This is repeated rhythmically and with regularity until the passage phase is concluded.

Even horses with fast moving legs need a certain amount of time for each progress of motion. Thus, while the hind leg of the diagonal touches the ground, takes up weight and flexes in the joints, the other hind leg needs to bridge the same space of time during the much easier motion upwards. This results in the required delayed suspension moment of the diagonal pair of legs that are not on the ground.

Potential conflicts between horse and rider, which initially occur because the inexperienced horse, depending on its temperament, will push out, forwards from the frame allocated to it, or lose tension, will require a flexible adaptation of the applied aids as in the piaffe. Depending on circumstances, under very fast changing conditions the half-halt will initially need to dominate during one stride and then the forward-driving leg aid, until the horse is once more in balance in the centre of its frame and starts to execute the passage independently and with regularity.

The goal is a rhythmic, diagonally alternating, energetic lifting off and touching down on the ground of both diagonal pairs of legs, which pushes the weight of the rider and horse vertically upward during the moment of the phase of suspension because of the lack of allowed spatial range.

This basic form of the passage, offered by the horse itself, allows the rider to blend more and more into the background, where he only needs to see to an improved execution of the movement with ever lighter aids. To achieve this the horse needs to push itself together and collect itself even further in order to maintain and improve the necessary elasticity for the increasingly high "flight curve". During the landing phase it becomes broader in its torso, which swings from side to side in rhythm with the alternating stepping diagonal pairs of legs. This swinging motion magically draws the loosely placed rider's legs to the horse's side and they swing rhythmically along the horse's body so that during the moment of lift-off during which the leg drives the horse forward, the aid is applied almost automatically. So basically, the horse picks up its impulsion by itself.

Conclusion of the movement

The different combinations of aids that can be applied to conclude the passage are determined by whether the horse subsequently comes to a halt, walks on, or is supposed to do the transition to the piaffe.

In order to complete the transition to a walk or a collected trot, it is sufficient in most cases to drive the horse forward less in the last landing phase, to keep the horse on the ground with the corresponding half-halts, and to extend the frame by lengthening the reins and giving with both hands, to such an extent that the horse can stretch itself. For the transition to walk, the rider will allow a distinctly larger frame so that the inherent tension and cadence of the passage collapses very quickly. Any further motion at the trot is stopped by suitable half-halts which are met by most horses with a composed walk. The rider needs to be sure to follow the nodding movement of the horse's head with his hands.

In order to change to the collected trot, the rider holds up the horse again, before the phase of suspension has collapsed completely, and thereby takes a small amount of the cadence into the collection, so that this becomes more elevated as time goes by.

The transition from the passage to the medium trot or the extended trot is in fact not much more complicated. After all, the foundation of the passage motion was the initial lift-off of the diagonal pair of legs, which is similar to the start of an increase in tempo at the trot; the curve of the phase of suspension was merely redirected upward. Therefore, for the transition to the trot, the horse's frame is simply enlarged without any change to the elevation and by maintaining the forward-driving aids so that the flight curve is flattened again and is lengthened forwards.

The transition from the passage to the piaffe counts as one of the most complicated transitions in dressage. Due to the complete omission of the phase of suspension, the piaffe is the exact opposite of the passage where the phase of suspension should be distinctly pronounced. Therefore, the transition to the piaffe always begins with the application of half-halts, during which the phase of suspension is continuously reduced until it is no longer present. The rider's legs in the forward-driving position at the front on the girth "lie in wait" for this moment in order that, through their aids, they may continue to maintain the trot-like motion, now without the phase of suspension and on the spot.

Evaluation

The passage gives the expert observer an idea about the degree of achievable cadence and collection, and the attained feeling of balance, shown by the horse. It demonstrates clearly to what extent the haunches are capable of taking up the weight and pushing it forwards and upwards again energetically. The leverage action of the forearms gives inferences regarding the aptitude of the horse for advanced dressage. The passage also gives indications regarding the precision of the rider's aids.

Critical moments

As in the case of many collective exercises, during which the forward-driving aids need to work in co-ordination against the retaining aids, the critical phase of the passage is most likely to be during the initial phase, when both aids meet each other. During the passage especially, the focal points of the applied aids can change astonishingly quickly from one stride to the next – in particular in the case of insufficient condition of the horse or difficult ground conditions. Young or nervous riders who do not yet have the necessary schooling and experience then often react too abruptly and start to counter the vehement thrust of the hind legs with correspondingly rough rein aids. In the long term however, only the aids applied in the correct way, corresponding to the horse's form on the day and the psychological state of the horse, will let the passage mature to one of the most valuable tools to give the horses in this schooling phase the "final polish".

Achievable degree of skill

The passage is a completely independent movement that can hardly be compared to any other exercise. The achievable degree of skill, therefore, lies predominantly in an optimised execution and the related increase of elasticity and strength of muscles. This will naturally also find its result in more expressive extensions at the trot, which are given distinctly more expression by the pushing force acquired through the passage.

Faults and corrections

While in the case of incorrectly ridden piaffes it is just about possible for the rider to sit out the trot-like movements, and thereby badly trained riders are tempted to carry out endless repetitions, the seating comfort in the case of faulty passages tends to be zero. That should be the reason why such riders avoid performing the passage in the same way as the medium or the extended trot or any other movement which comes with a distinct development of impulsion (Schwung).

In horses with too tight strides, the back activity is limited to such an extent that in the passage they can only demonstrate tensed-up strides with insufficiently lowered hindquarters.

Lack of regularity

The passage is meant to completely train the ability of the horse regarding cadence. The cadence also includes the regular beat of all four legs. While most horses don't let even energetic riders confuse them too much during the phase of support, the diagonal pair of legs is very susceptible to disturbances of every kind during the phase of suspension.

All distortions, tension, and other types of resistance will inevitably lead to motion disturbances and thereby also cause lack of regularity. In addition, irregularities in the application of the aids, weight distribution and rein contact, as well as a badly fitted saddle or bit, can also disturb the rhythm as they usually influence the motion processes differently on each side, where they would normally be the same.

During the passage, such riders usually cause a lack of regularity by applying whip aids during the flexion phase – especially if they gesticulate in the area of the hocks with schooling whips that are too long. Thereby, the horse is forced to pull up the suspended leg even further and thus rest on the other hind leg for longer, so that the lack of regularity appears intensified. The horse seems to be lame and sometimes carries out stringhalt-like movements.

In order to correct this, all faults that result from tension of any kind, lack of chewing on the bit, lack of control in the poll region, and similar faults initially need to be eliminated. It is also important to apply the forward-driving aids in such a way that they are respected by the horse executing the passage, and therefore do not have to be applied anew for each trotting stride. Thus, the aids need to lead to a better co-operation with the horse, which will allow the rider to be more reserved.

Experienced riders are certainly capable of having their own positive influence on any lack of co-operation of their horses during the passage. For all other riders it is advised that before attempting the highly sensitive passage tours they improve the working morale of their horses so that they become more independent and industrious in the exercise and no longer force the rider to constantly intervene.

Tense steps

During the passage, the hind legs, which are placed well under the horse in the case of well-flexed hocks, have the effect of shock absorbers that flex downwards under the weight and then push straight forwards and upward again with regularity and energy. Despite all the inherent tension of this exercise, this requires the absolute relaxation of the hocks and the back.

Despite the spatial scope, which needs to be greatly restricted during the passage, the horse needs to remain soft in the poll and mouth in order to continue to want to step forwards at the same time. Unfortunately, flexed hocks and hind legs placed well under the horse's body are becoming rarer all the time. Quite often you can observe horses which move in stilt-like slow motion with stiff front and hind legs, similar to the action of a stork. The stiff back of the horse, which is flung upward from the non-elastic hind legs, catapults the rider from the saddle and uncompromisingly uncovers all schooling faults that the rider was able to conceal to a certain degree in other movements.

In order to maintain some sort of contact with the saddle, these riders cling on to the horse with reins and knees or push themselves off in the stirrups. Naturally this seat does not permit any differentiated, sensitive aids, leads to significant impairments of the back work of the horse, and is responsible for almost all faults listed. Some saddle manufacturers have reacted to this and are making money hand over fist by producing ever-larger knee and leg pads.

From the viewpoint of the horse, any other than the illustrated form of motion is no longer possible under these circumstances. The far too cramped neck, which causes difficulty in breathing and significant pain in the area of the parotid gland, has a downward lever action on the back in the area which carries the saddle, and the stiff hind legs push in the other direction and push the croup upward. The tightened back bent concave in this manner is incapable of any motion, leads to a kind of "elevator effect", and the round, high wave-like motion required resembles instead the peaked deflections of a seismograph.

The corrective options are the result of the fault listed above: if a too tensed-up neck restricts the active back of the horse to such an extent, the fault can only be improved through an enlarged frame in conjunction with a more pronounced tendency to move forwards. Half-halts that are accepted by a supple horse allow almost any rider to carry the hands forwards and thereby allow the neck more space. Only then will the increasingly forward-driving aids show the necessary success without squeezing the horse back together into a tight frame. Accordingly as a preparation for performing the passage, the rider needs to ensure good Durchlässigkeit (suppleness) by riding all forms of transitions right from the start of a training session.

In stubborn cases it is recommended to execute the passage on curved lines such as, for example, on a volte or serpentine, which require a frequent re-positioning of the neck. In this way it is actually possible to get every horse to drop its neck and to round its back.

Swaying passage

If the impulsion created during the passage is not let out sufficiently at the front it will search for another direction and deviate to the side. Thus, the hind legs no longer push the horse straight forwards upward in the direction of the bit, but to the left and right of it. The horse usually swings over the shoulder of the front leg, which is currently in the flexion phase, and forces the riders to collapse from one hip to the other or swing in tune with the upper body.

Horses that energetically and unflaggingly move forwards and develop sufficient impulsion, even when their riders impede them to an extraordinary extent, are particularly susceptible to this fault. Thus impulsion is present – it merely moves in the incorrect direction. Therefore, the corrective measure in this case is not really too difficult for professional riders: a distinct improvement of the control of the poll region and Durchlässigkeit (suppleness) allows the rider to slightly extend the frame until the horse starts to push itself forwards in a straight line. In stubborn cases, the rider's legs can check the swaying shoulders through timely, energetic application at the front on the girth and push them forwards.

Dragging hind legs

It is difficult to correct dragging hind legs because here we have to deal with a total lack of impulsion. On the one side are horses which are disadvantaged for anatomical reasons. On the other side, however, are

Dragging hind legs in the passage are often a sign of a missing completion of the thrust phase and defects in the activity of the horse's back.

horses which in particular have been robbed of their options of motion and thus have resigned themselves accordingly. They lead their riders to believe they are in a passage-like state through regularly recurring interruptions to the progress of motion by long delayed suspension phases of one diagonal pair of legs. An exaggerated support phase and a lack of a thrust phase lead to the hind legs dragging. In extreme cases the horse gives the impression that it is clawing the ground with the supporting diagonal pair of legs while its drags the other diagonal pair over the ground.

It is rare for the rider to be able to correct this horse merely by applying lively forward-driving aids. On the contrary, the causes that have led to the abnormal motion process need to be found and thoroughly eliminated first. Often a tight, tensed-up back and much too tight a neck position play the deciding roles and it is common that these defects have been consolidated over years and can be followed like a thread through all movements. Often such horses also have a tendency to rush or run in the medium trot or extended trot because they do not want to relax their tight or damaged back. Without doing so however, it is impossible for them to extend the length of the individual strides.

Only if the trainer manages to set up the horse in a lower position and ride it over the back through corrective measures and diversified exercises such as cavalletti work, frequent hacking out, jumping of small fences, free jumping and suchlike, can an improvement be achieved. However, it is a long and difficult road to introduce the newly developed impulsion and the more lively motion process into the passage, which should be executed only very rarely.

In the case of horses for which this poor motion process can be followed back merely to learning errors or a lack of co-operation, short passage tours from the walk or from the piaffe have proven themselves as extraordinarily good corrective measures. It is less recommended to initiate the passage from the trot owing to the domineering rein aids.

Remarks

In the case of supple horses which co-operate well and which are fundamentally used to reacting immediately to the aids of the rider, hardly any problems will therefore occur in the development of the passage. It is important however that the understanding rider leaves himself further sufficient time and takes care not to overtax his horse's strength. The most important aim for the rider therefore remains the continued exercising of his horse – not the execution of the movement as such.

Literature

The manual of horsemanship, 10th Edition
Published by the British Horse Society, 2002

Dressage for the 21st Century, Paul Belasik
Published by J. A. Allen, 2002

Elements of dressage, Kurd Albrecht von Ziegner
Published by CADMOS Equestrian, 2002

Training the horse in hand, Alfons J. Dietz
Published by CADMOS Equestrian, 2004

CADMOS

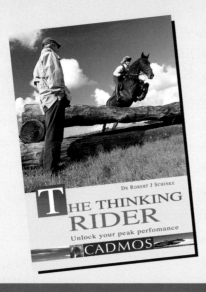

Dr Robert J Schinke
THE THINKING RIDER

Since writing this popluar book Focused Riding, Dr Robert Schinke has devoted much time and study to the many aspects of mental sports coaching. In his own words: "My views have both refined and altered with time. Now I propose that anyone wishing to integrate sport psychology techniques looks for answers using a wider repertoire of skills."

It is these skills that he covers in this book. With chapters devoted to sport confidence, optimism, emotional management, and performance perspectives, he provides practical techniques that will be of use to every rider from the aspiring national competitor to the recreational rider and his or her coach.

For the last ten years Dr Schinke has worked with national team and professional sport affiliates in Canada and abroad.

160 pages, hardback
ISBN 978-3-86127-917-4

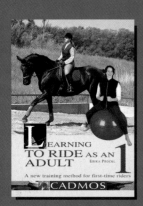

Erika Prockl
LEARNING TO RIDE AS AN ADULT 1

This book contains a new training method for first-time riders.
Erika Prockl is a teacher in further education and a certified riding instructor.
"Learning to ride as an adult 1" should be required reading for every riding instructor and adult novice rider.

128 pages, hardback
ISBN 978-3-86127-908-2

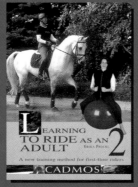

Erika Prockl
LEARNING TO RIDE AS AN ADULT 2

This second volume of "Learning to ride as an adult" is a modern manual of riding and movement instructions for riders with ambition, who want to ride their horse free of tension, with momentum, via the seat and with light aids.

128 pages, hardback
ISBN 978-3-86127-912-9

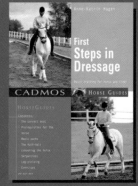

Anne-Katrin Hagen
FIRST STEPS IN DRESSAGE

Dressage involves drawing out the natural capability of the horse and shaping it into something beautiful and expressive. The horse must learn how to balance under the rider and move in elegant self-carriage.
Anne-Katrin Hagen is an accomplished dressage trainer.

32 pages, paperback
ISBN 978-3-86127-932-7

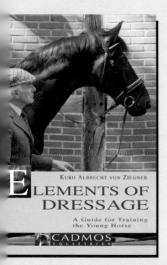
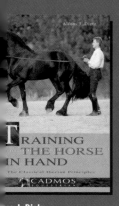
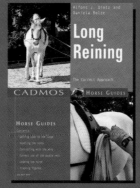
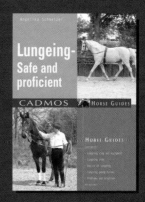

CADMOS
Equestrian

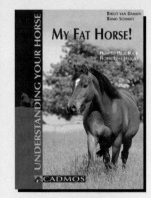

Cathy Tindall/Jaki Bell
SHIATSU FOR YOUR HORSE

In recent years the benefits of massage, physiotherapy and other 'touch' therapies to horses have become much better appreciated. Shiatsu is a traditional Japanese therapy based on pressure and stretches, the benefits of which you can share with your horse, enhancing his well-being and happiness. This book is required reading for any horse owner or rider who wants to give something back to these amazing, sensitive and understanding animals.

144 pages, hardback
ISBN 978-3-86127-915-0

Birgit van Damsen/Romo Schmidt
MY FAT HORSE!

Overweight horses are no rarity nowadays. Ponies and native breeds are often too heavy and are prone to weight related ailments. This book looks at the causes of obesity, and how to recognise it. It explains the dangers of obesity and offers solutions on how to reduce excess weight, examining diet, exercise and pasture management.
Birgit van Damsen is a journalist specialised in equine subjects and the author of several horse books.

80 pages, paperback
ISBN 978-3-86127-913-6

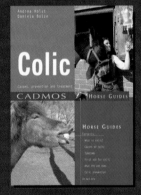

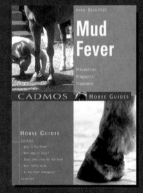

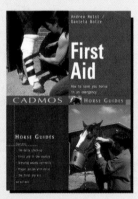

Andrea Holst/Daniela Bolze
COLIC

Colic is one of the main reasons for calling out the vet. It is a disease that must not be taken lightly, as it often proves fatal.
This book explains the causes of colic, the symptoms of the various colic types – of which there are many – and particularly how to prevent colic. This is something every horse owner should know, because most colics can be prevented.

32 pages, paperback
ISBN 978-3-86127-945-7

Anke Rüsbüldt
MUD FEVER

Mud fever is the term given to a serious skin ailment affecting the back of the pastern and heel area of horses. In this book Anke Rüsbüldt details how to recognise mud fever, how it can be prevented through correct equine care and management and how to successfully treat the condition when it does occur.
Anke Rüsbüldt is an equine veterinarian and the author of many specialist equine titles.

32 pages, paperback
ISBN 978-3-86127-935-8

Andrea Holst/Daniela Bolze
FIRST AID

Every rider should be prepared for an emergency. This guide describes how to treat the most frequent injuries and illnesses that occur, when to call the vet and what to do until the vet arrives.
The authors describe how to bandage a wound in an emergency, what should be observed in the daily inspection for soundness, and much more.

32 pages, paperback
ISBN 978-3-86127-940-2

Cadmos Equestrian
171 GordonRoad   Nunhead
GB - London SE15 3RT
Tel.: 02074 504117   Fax: 08701 367219